LEVEL UP

LEVEL UP

ELEVATE YOUR GAME & CRUSH YOUR GOALS

ALYSON
VAN HOOSER

To Willow, Lincoln, and Duke.

For all the nights you cuddled up beside me on the couch while I wrote, I hope this book helps you crush your goals and supports you in reaching your dreams.

Published and Distributed by
SOUND WISDOM
PO Box 310
Shippensburg, PA 17257-0310
717-530-2122

info@soundwisdom.com

www.soundwisdom.com

Cover design by Eileen Rockwell

ISBN 13 TP: 978-1-64095-197-6

ISBN 13 eBook: 978-1-64095-198-3

For Worldwide Distribution, Printed in the U.S.A.

4 5 6 / 23

CONTENTS

INTRODUCTION **13**

    #StraightUp 16

    #WhatReallyMatters 17

    #TheDifferentiator 18

    #YouDecide 19

PART 1   **OWN YOUR PERSPECTIVE.** **21**

CHAPTER 1   **THE OWNERSHIFT** **25**

    #OwnIt 26

    #GetYourMindRight 30

    #NewWhip 32

    #Curved. 33

CHAPTER 2   **LAY DOWN THE LAW.** **37**

    #LayDownTheLaw 39

    #DoItAgain. 41

    #LawsNotRules 42

    #HowTo 43

CHAPTER 3   **YOU ~~DESERVE~~ EARN IT**. **49**

　　　　　　　#LifesABeach *51*

　　　　　　　#IsItWorthItLetMeEarnIt. *53*

　　　　　　　#OffTrack. *54*

　　　　　　　#LifesNotFair. *56*

CHAPTER 4   **NO EXCUSES** **57**

　　　　　　　#FigureItOut *58*

　　　　　　　#ChokeThemOut *60*

　　　　　　　#WhatsYourExcuse *62*

PART 2   **OWN YOUR AWARENESS** **65**

CHAPTER 5   **STEALTH SKILL** **69**

　　　　　　　#WinnersAdapt *70*

　　　　　　　#SelfAbandoned *70*

　　　　　　　#StayTrue *72*

　　　　　　　#RestaurantLife *75*

CHAPTER 6   **MOTIVATION** **79**

　　　　　　　#MotivationTheory. *80*

　　　　　　　#WhatsGoingOn *83*

CHAPTER 7   **GENERATIONS** **87**

　　　　　　　#5Generations. *88*

　　　　　　　#ThingsChange *96*

CHAPTER 8   **GET ON MY LEVEL** **99**

CHAPTER 9   **S.E.E. CLEARLY** **105**

CHAPTER 10   **CATCH & CRUSH** **109**

　　　　　　　#OwnYourEI. *110*

　　　　　　　#CatchTheFeeling *113*

　　　　　　　#CrushTheFeeling *116*

#CrushYourGoals .117

#IDecide 119

PART 3   OWN YOUR ACTIONS 121

CHAPTER 11   BE FOR YOU, NOT AGAINST YOU 125

#Knowledge. 126

#MakeTime 127

#PersonalGoals 127

#ProfessionalGoals 130

#DreamingInExperience. 131

#LearningInTheWait. 132

#Strength 134

#BreakdownToBreakthrough 134

#Spirit 137

#JustGoWithIt 139

#RosetoEffect 140

#Saturday 141

#BeYourChampion. 142

CHAPTER 12   FAIL UP. 145

#EntryLevel 145

#FessUpToFailUp. .150

#Unlocked 153

#KillMeNow 153

#FailureIsOpportunity 155

CHAPTER 13   SALTY OR SUCCESSFUL 157

#ItsFunnyBecauseItsTrue 157

#BeAuthentic 160

#KeepUpYourEndOfTheDeal 162

#KnowYourAudience 162

#Appearance360 164

#FaceToFace 165

#ThinkActLookLikeAPro 165

#OnlineAppearance 171

CHAPTER 14   **GET IT TOGETHER** **175**

#WorkDontWish 176

#BGBoard 178

#QuittingTime 182

#RadicallyExecute .184

CHAPTER 15   **EMPOWER OTHERS** **185**

#HomeForTheSummer 185

#EasyGiving 187

#HurtsSoGood 188

#DeepSacrifice 189

#HowMuchToGive .190

#MassiveImpact 192

CHAPTER 16   **BE BOLD** **193**

#BoldMoves 194

#OwnYourOpportunity 196

#ItDidntWork 200

#WhyNot 202

CHAPTER 17   **BYE FELICIA** **203**

#GetOverYourself .204

#RootIssue 205

#BeTheSolution 207

CHAPTER 18   **NOT THIRSTY, JUST THRIVING** **209**

#MemoryLane 210

#YourRelationshipWithYourself 212

#HowDoYouNetwork 213

#NotAwkwardJustImpressive 217

CHAPTER 19 MAKE YOUR OWN HYPE *219*

#Hype 220

#CleanHouse 221

#ItFactor 223

#KeepYourWord 224

CONCLUSION **227**

#YourTurn 228

Acknowledgments **231**

Meet Alyson Van Hooser **237**

Contact Alyson 239

Connect with Alyson on Social 239

INTRODUCTION

Everything you envision for yourself can be yours.

But first, you have to own it.

I know firsthand the necessity of owning the responsibility to create great things for yourself in life. Growing up, my family could hardly afford food or heat, so anything my siblings or I wanted, we had to figure out a creative way to get. In my small town, we have a spring clean-up day every year where everyone in the city limits puts their junk out by the curb. There would be couches, mattresses, toys—things you could not even imagine. People would put it out one day, and the next day the City Public Works Department would haul it off to the dump. As kids, my brother and sister and I were excited about this day every year—not because we were going to clean out our house, but because hopefully someone would put something out that we had been wanting! When someone left something out by the curb, it was free game. They did not care who came and got it...as long as it was gone! We would get lucky time and time again, finding things like bicycles, basketballs, and furniture. It was better than Christmas for us most years!

I remember specifically one year where my brother found an all-in-one record, radio, and cassette player in someone's pile. The stereo was huge, but he carried it all the way home. He set it up in his bedroom, and as much as I wanted to listen to the stereo too, he said it was off-limits for me. Several months later, my brother moved out and he didn't take that stereo with him, so it became mine.

As a 13-year-old girl, I wore out that stereo. On Friday nights, I would record the *Top 9 at 9* radio countdown on a cassette tape. First thing Saturday morning when I got up, I would rush into my brother's bedroom and listen to the tape I recorded so I could learn all the lyrics to big hits like "In Da Club" by 50 Cent and "All I Have" by J.Lo. I don't know about you, but my ability to remember multiple song lyrics from my childhood far outweighs my ability to remember things as an adult—like where I put my keys or why I opened the refrigerator!

At 13, learning these songs was serious business—so I made a plan. Almost as soon as I woke up, I would make sure that my little sister was settled watching TV in the living room and that the front door was locked. Then I would tuck myself away in my brother's room so I could concentrate on the music.

More often than I can count, I would get interrupted. Not by my little sister, but by a knock at the front door. Nobody else but she and I were home, so I would have to answer it. I would pull back the old blanket hanging over the bedroom window so I could see if I knew who was at the door. I usually did—typically it was the preacher from down the road. I would run to the living room and open the door just enough to peek my head out. I did not want him to see the conditions in which we lived. He was a nice, white-haired man with a Southern drawl somewhere between Matthew McConaughey and Barney Fife. He was funny and kind, and I liked him. But it would not be only him at the door.

The preacher would smile and laughingly say something like, "You recognize this guy?"

At 13, I was not sure exactly what to say, so I would just smile. Of course I recognized *this guy*; it was my dad.

"Found this guy wandering the streets, figured I'd bring him home," the preacher would say.

Standing there holding the door as if this were my own house, as if I were the one in charge of it all at just 13 years old, I would stand back and let my dad walk through the front door. I want you to know that my dad is a good man, but he has struggled with the demon of addiction for my entire life. I knew why he had been out all night. I had seen how drugs would make him a completely different person, someone who could not think or operate rationally. He would come in and fall asleep on the couch, and I would go back to my cassette player.

Although that situation may seem alarming, this was just another normal day in my life growing up. Through all of these "normal" days, I learned to be resourceful because I had no resources. I learned that I can do anything if I make a plan and take action. I learned that I cannot control other people's choices, but I can control my reactions. I learned that life is not easy, but I have the choice to focus on the positive.

Years of living in poverty, without a mother, neglected by my father...my experiences did not shake me; they shaped me. It became my natural instinct to step up to the plate and take responsibility for making my life turn out better than anything I had known before. And I did. And I am writing this book **for you** so that you can too.

From as early as I can remember, I have spent time studying the root causes of success and failure—the behaviors, attitudes, and traits that distinguish high achievers. Over the past several years, I finally have been able to see clearly through all the noise of life and straight to the *"it" factor* that separates those who get what they want from those who don't. What is it? Ownership. Taking responsibility for who you are, what you do, and what your life will become.

Despite only recently being able to name it, I can look back, even as early as eight years old, and see that I realized the power of *owning it*. I recognized that I could control my life if I chose to put my stake in the ground and do something. This mindset is, and has been, the foundation of all the lessons I have learned throughout my life. Leveling up and owning it is the only foolproof success strategy.

> ## Leveling up and owning it is the only foolproof success strategy.

#StraightUp

I know you're just barely into the intro of this book and I am already coming at you full throttle, but I believe to my core that when you realize your purpose, you have to go all in and all out to maximize your calling.

I want you to know that if you and I met on the street, you would quickly see that I am laid-back, a little quirky, and always looking for a reason to laugh. But, straight up…when we get down to talking about changing your life, I get intense. Why? Because there is so much at stake for you, me, and everyone else who is trying to do something, get something, be something in this one chance at life we all get. Only one chance! So, I am not going to play around. This is not just a book full of entertaining stories for you to enjoy. It is meant to help you clearly recognize what you have to do to change your life. As you dig into the pages of this book, so much of the thought processes and action steps we will discuss will cross over perfectly for personal life applications, but my focus in this book is on professional success.

Most people have goals, but very few people ever achieve them. Why? Because most people do not understand the steps they need to take or the shifts they need to implement in order to make success happen for them. I don't want that to be your story! So, I am here for those of you who know deep down in your gut that you want more. I'm here for those of you whom I have met, whom I know, whom I would recognize, resonate, and relate with on the street, in the living room, in the office, and in the boardroom. The people who never had anything but are dreaming of everything. The young people entering the work world and searching for how to start their career off on the right foot. The men and women grinding it out every day at work but wanting so badly to be more valued and get to the next level. The individuals with the side hustles because their souls are starving for something different than what they have now. The people who have been beaten down, held back, and haven't—yet!—been able to rise above. This book is for those people—my people—who are looking for the nitty-gritty details of what they need to do to gain respect, opportunity, and harness the power to drive their own success and crush goal after goal after goal.

#WhatReallyMatters

We are going to dig deep into what it is that you really want in this life and how you are going to get it. I hope, with every fiber of my being, that what you want is more significant than any material thing and more meaningful than superficial concerns. I hope that your goals will feed your soul, not your ego. I hope that your dreams reach far beyond you and touch the lives of the people around you right now and for generations into the future. We are all supposed to leave our mark on this earth. No one else can leave *your* mark; it is yours to give or withhold. You can choose to do nothing to reach your potential and live out your purpose, or you can choose to take ownership of your gifts and responsibilities, crush your goals, and leave a legacy. For you, right now...I think it is time for a massive breakthrough. It is time for you to *level up and own it*!

#TheDifferentiator

This book is divided into three parts based on the three responsibilities you need to own in order to control your life and crush your goals.

Part One: Own your perspective.

Most people accept their default perspective. What I see most often is that a person's perspective is at the heart of what is holding them back from positive change in their life. Your perspective sets the tone for everything you will and will not accomplish, and you have to make sure that you get yours right. It took me growing up in a really tough environment to realize that I needed to shift my perspective and intentionally own the responsibility of making my life what I wanted it to be. I am sharing my stories so that you do not have to have a breakdown to have your breakthrough. When you take responsibility for who you are and the mindset required to become successful, you will shift your perspective to one that catapults you to the place you want to go. Part One sets the stage for Parts Two and Three, because you have to understand your mindset in order to equip and inspire yourself and others to take action.

Part Two: Own your awareness.

Owning it includes increasing your understanding of yourself and the people around you. When you understand what makes other people tick, what motivates them to take action, and how their minds work, then you can figure out exactly what you need to do to be successful for the rest of your life. Equally as important—when you have the same awareness about yourself, then you create the internal catalyst required for your future success. The information in Part Two is critical for working successfully through Part Three, because the skills discussed in this section will enable you to adapt and take precise action for yourself and those around you.

Part Three: Own your actions.

Part Three is your no-fluff, no-filler, nitty-gritty, practical action plan for success. The tactics described in Part Three are where the rubber meets the road. We discuss the specific steps you can take to transform your professional life. These are decisions and actions anyone can do but very few people will. Owning your actions may be hard, but it is not impossible. It simply involves choosing to be intentional about how you handle yourself and interact with others.

#YouDecide

Your actions and reactions to situations in your life either create a road to your dream destiny or take you down a path to mediocrity or even self-destruction. Ultimately, you decide whether you hit home runs or whether you just let everything hit the fan.

Everybody wants the promise of success, but few are willing to go through the process. Owning it will take work on your part. But when you choose to own it, the world will take notice and reward you for it. Very few people are audacious enough not to let anything stand in their way of achieving their goals, but I have a feeling you are in that minority.

We are not doing motivational hype here. As you apply the wisdom in the pages to your life, you are going to transform your mind, increase your knowledge, and be pointed directly toward results-producing action. This book offers you a strategic game plan for how you should approach life so you can get *what* you want and get *where* you want to be. Get ready! Because when you choose to *level up and own it*, you start killing it.

> **Ultimately, you decide whether you hit home runs or whether you just let everything hit the fan.**

PART 1

OWN YOUR
PERSPECTIVE

For you to start positively changing your life, you have to own your perspective. Your perspective sets the tone for every single aspect of who you are, what you do, and what you will accomplish, so it is critical that you get this right. Owning your perspective simply means that you are putting everything in your mind in the right place, on the right track. If your perspective is off, you will not get the results you want in life.

Now, maybe you already have everything in life figured out. It is possible, but I doubt that's the case. Not because you are not smart, experienced, and resourceful, but because most people operate on apathy and do not take time to make sure their perspective is right.

Think about your entire life. Have you ever taken the time to sit down and dig deep into yourself and analyze your psyche in order to make sure your perspective is right? If your answer is no, then buckle up, buttercup—we're about to go on a life-changing ride. Part One is the heart of where owning it starts. You either control your perspective or you willingly give up control to someone or something else. When you control it, you own it. When you own it, you can make things happen for yourself. Your success rides on your willingness to show up right now and take this seriously. We are changing your perspective to one that will transform your life. Let's get down to business.

> *You either control your perspective or you willingly give up control to someone or something else.*

CHAPTER 1

THE OWNERSHIFT

For as long as I can remember, I have been hungry.

Physically hungry as a kid sometimes, yes, but more than that, I have always had this hunger deep in my soul to live out a purpose that is so much bigger than what society would say someone in my shoes should be aiming for.

Have you had that feeling of knowing you were meant for more? Have you felt the pull toward greatness despite society expecting less out of you? Or perhaps you've experienced the itch to make something of yourself, but you lack the motivation, energy, or knowhow to take steps in the right direction. Maybe that is you right now. The thing is, you can have that hunger, that burning desire, or that small voice impelling you to live your value, but that feeling alone will not get you any closer to crushing your goals. You have to take action…and by *action* I mean correct, calculated, and consistent action—right now. That is your only option for success.

The Three Cs of Owned Actions

✔ Correct
✔ Calculated
✔ Consistent

The first correct, calculated action you must take is to establish a firm, strong, dependable, error-free foundation on which you will consistently rely from this point forward. That foundation is your **perspective** because everything in your life is built on the way you see yourself and the world around you.

In order to get your foundation right, you have to make sure every piece is positioned correctly. If one aspect is off, everything built on top of it will eventually crumble; all of it will be meaningless in your journey toward success. Getting your perspective right is critical for your success, and I am betting that since you have made it this far into the book, you are like me—you *want* to get this right! You do not have time to waste messing around with trial and error. You want answers! You want results! Okay, so let's dig into what got me to where I am so we can get you to where you want to be.

#OwnIt

Most little kids do not spend time thinking about how to create a better life for themselves. But while I was watching VH1's *Pop-Up Video* as an eight-year-old kid in my bedroom, I was thinking about what life could and should be like, and I was figuring out what I had to do to get there. And I did.

My mother chose to leave our family when I was in primary school, so I grew up with my dad, older brother, and younger sister. We lived off a Social Security Disability check and government food stamps. Both came at the beginning of every month, but neither lasted long enough to provide for the four of us. Because of my dad's drug addiction, the money we got would go out as fast as it came in. Every month we ran out of money. During my childhood, it was not uncommon to wake up to my dad panicking because the service men had come to turn off our electricity or water. More often than not, by the end of the month we would be left with bare cabinets, and all of us would be counting down the days until he would get his next check.

As a child, I remember feeling a need to hide my massive anxiety and a constant awareness of my family's strained financial situation. I kept thinking about not only myself, but my older brother and younger sister. I chose to smile and laugh on the outside, but on the inside I was operating in survival mode. I would think to myself over and over again that we could not keep living this way…month to month, sometimes day to day, wondering if our basic needs would be met. I wanted something better for us.

I finally decided that I could not control what my parents did or did not do, but *I could control me*. I could choose not to sit idle anymore while someone else's selfish, apathetic decision-making hurt me, my sister, and my brother. I stepped up and took responsibility for making things better for all of us. I owned it. So, at a young age I got involved in my family's "financial planning." I got involved in a way that might seem unorthodox, but as a child in survival mode, I felt it was the only solution to a problem that absolutely needed to be fixed.

I would wait for the day when the government check came, knowing that I would have to take immediate action. When night came, I would lie in the bed I shared with my little sister—wide awake—listening and waiting for the eerie calm that would eventually come over the house. The TV in the living room would be blaring Monday night wrestling or some strange sci-fi show, but beyond the noise of the TV I could sense when there was nothing else going on in the house. I could identify when my brother and sister had fallen asleep. I knew when my dad had finally passed out. That was when I had to make a choice. I could lie there and do nothing, or I could take action to make things better for the family. I chose to own it.

I would slide out from under the covers carefully so as not to wake up my sister, tiptoe out of my bed, and make my way to the door. Peeking around the edge of my door and down the hallway, I would listen for sounds and signs of movement from my dad. I recall the darkness of the hallway punctuated only by the flashing blue glow from the TV as the images changed. It was a scary scene to me as a little girl, but I knew that I had to navigate through it for the good of my family.

Making my way down to the end of the hall, I would stop and crouch down. Just barely peeking around the corner of the wall into the dark living room, I could see from the light of the TV and the fog of cigarette smoke that my dad was home, but because of his addiction, he was not really there. He was sitting on the couch, hunched over, with his eyes closed and his burning cigarette dangling tenuously between his fingers.

I would take a deep breath and then move into the living room. I remember feeling so nervous. It seemed like someone had turned up the volume on everything…the TV, my pounding heart, my dad's breathing. I had to remind myself over and over in my head that I was taking action now to fix the problem of empty cabinets later. A few quick steps around the corner, and I had made it to the coffee table by the couch where he lay. His wallet, cigarettes, lighter, and drink were all sitting there on the edge. I grabbed his wallet and opened it up. Gently sliding out one 20-dollar bill, I quickly closed his wallet, laid it back down by his ashtray, and ran as fast as I could back to my room.

It always felt like a close call, but every time I made it back safely to my room. I tucked the money away in the very back of my drawer and crawled back into bed beside my sister. Sometimes the anxiety of wondering if what I was doing was right or wrong would keep me up for hours. But there was also a feeling of the weight being lifted off my shoulders for just a little bit.

Looking back, I never recall my dad noticing there was less money in his wallet the next day. But I vividly remember my dad's relief at the end of the month, when the cabinets got empty and a 20-dollar bill would appear in his wallet, a token from another late-night mission into the living room.

Because I was dealt a hand of cards in life where I had to figure out how to survive as a child, I learned that if you *level up* and choose to own the responsibility to make good things happen in your life, then you can change your situation to match your dreams.

My choice to own the responsibility for who I am and who I will become has licensed me to crush goal after goal and get opportunities personally, civically, and especially professionally that I never would have received otherwise. Because none of us are guaranteed tomorrow, now is the time for you to level up and get the life you want. In order for this to work, you have to put your stake in the ground and never go back. You have to own it regardless of the circumstances, even when…

> …you should not have to

> …it gets hard

> …it gets scary

> …you are unsure

Owning it will transform how you operate from this moment forward. I know this may be a complete 180-degree shift for you—something unlike anything you have ever done before. It may not come naturally. It may not be easy. But it will be empowering, freeing, and positively life-changing if you decide to get this mental shift right.

#GetYourMindRight

Your perspective starts forming at birth, but you do not have to accept what has become your default.

Scientists have discovered that you literally do not have the full power of the frontal lobe of your brain—the part that helps with reasoning, planning and judgment—until you are in your mid-20s.[1] So, if you haven't done a complete check of your perspective since you were 25 to make sure you have got it right, then your critical foundation could be unsteady.

In order to make sure you get your perspective in line with the *owning it* mindset, you have to get brutally honest with yourself. Right now, this very moment, you have to figure out if you are owning it or not. You have to be willing to peel back the layers of your life so that you can determine what you are taking responsibility for and what you still need to take ownership of. You don't want to build your life on a flimsy foundation, right? Then let's get down to it.

There are two elements that drive your life story:

1. The way you think.

2. The way you act.

You might be thinking, *Only two elements, Alyson? That sounds too simple to be true.* I am telling you that it is true! In every situation you face in life, the way you think about it and the actions you take because of it will determine what you achieve.

What separates those who achieve what they want from those who do not? It is a question of whether they are owning it or not. There are two types of people in this world:

---

1 Mariam Arain et al., "Maturation of the Adolescent Brain," *Neuropsychiatric Disease and Treatment* 9 (2013): 449–61. doi: 10.2147/NDT.S39776.

1. Haves

2. Owners

You've probably heard the terms *Haves* and *Have Nots*. Most people want to be a Have, not a Have Not. But I am flipping the script on this one. I say there are *Haves* and *Owners*, and if you want a successful life, you do not want to be a Have; you want to be an Owner. Let's figure out where you are right now.

> ## You do not have to accept what has become your default.

We all start off as Haves, and the sad reality is that most people remain Haves for their entire life. Whether Haves realize it or not, they go through life with an apathetic approach. There is no clear intentional purpose, rhyme, or reason to how they think and act every day. When all is said and done, their one chance at life is wasted, and they are left with a lackluster existence compared to what they could have accomplished.

What is a telltale sign that you could be a Have? You believe that if you had more time, more money, more connections; or if you were smarter, better looking, more disciplined, etc., **then** you could finally reach your goals. At the end of the day, if you are a Have—more importantly, if you stay a Have—you most likely will not achieve all you are meant for, because someone or something else is pulling the strings that control your life. That is why if you are a Have, now is the time to make the Owner*shift*.

The Owners…these are my people! Owners do not just *have* the ability to think and act; they own it! They take full responsibility for their goals by thinking and acting with intentionality every moment, every day, and every week. Owners call the shots for what they accomplish. When it seems there is no other way to make something happen, Owners find a way. Owners take dreams and make them reality. Owners fall down and get back up. Owners do not give up; they give out. Owners do not wish and hope; they act.

Now, usually when I talk about Haves versus Owners, people tend to assume they are Owners when in reality they are not. I do not want you to be mistaken. Not because I want you to experience a tough realization, but because I want you to have a positive, life-changing revelation. You have to make sure you know exactly what foundation you are currently operating from. Let me give you a quick example to help further clarify the difference between Haves and Owners because it's crucial that you get this right.

#NewWhip

Up until my sophomore year of college, I did not own a vehicle. I could not afford one. I borrowed other people's vehicles and paid friends gas money to get a ride to school, work, home—wherever. The friends I commuted with back and forth to college all graduated after my freshman year, so I had to figure something out. I still had two years left of college and was going to be commuting 400-plus miles a week. It did not matter if it was going to be easy for me to afford a reliable vehicle or not; I had to buy one. My only criteria for a vehicle were that it had to be affordable and reliable.

After weeks of exploring financing options, I finally found a 2000 Chevy Impala that was perfect for me. The elderly lady who owned it had passed away, so her family was selling it dirt cheap to the first person who would take it off their hands. The car was already nine years old when I bought it, but it had only 60,000 miles on it. Of course that was great, but the fact that it had leather seats, a sunroof, and an upgraded sound system made me feel like I was on top of the world driving down the interstate.

As soon as I signed on the dotted line for the car loan at the bank, everyone congratulated me on *owning* my first car. As I relished my perceived freedom, I drove circles around town in my new-to-me car. But—hear me clearly—the point I want to make is that I *had* the car, but I did not *own* the car. I would not own the car until I paid off the loan at the bank. Until then, the bank actually owned the car and ultimately called the shots on what I could or could not do with it.

Because I didn't own the car, every month I had to show up and make payments to the bank. These payments had to occur on their timeline, not mine. I could not sell the car and get something better without letting them know and making sure the loan was paid off. I could not even wreck the car without getting the bank involved...because they owned it, not me. I don't know about you, but I don't like having to check in with someone or someplace in order to make a move in my life. I do not want someone else controlling my life. I am betting you don't either. But unless you choose to *own* your perspective, someone else will. If you do not choose to take responsibility for your life, then your life will be controlled by your family, your boss, your friends, your kids, your bad luck, your mistakes, and anything else that is not you.

#Curved

Curved: (slang) getting rejected or shut down

Right out of college I took a job that had endless future promise, but I knew it would be a grind in the meantime. Long hours, long commute, dirty work, little pay. I was starting at the very bottom, but I was there for it. Contrary to popular belief, there are young people out there today who are willing to pay their dues to earn success.

I got a phone call out of the blue one day from a well-respected leader in the community asking me to apply and interview for a management position in his business. Matt (not his real name) was a member of my church, where I had served by helping develop and lead the youth programs. I didn't know him well by any means, but apparently through my involvement with the church he was familiar with my character and work ethic.

After the conversation ended, I had an interview scheduled for a position that would almost double my current salary, essentially eliminate 70 minutes from my commute to and from work, and give me an awesome schedule conducive for a healthier work-life balance. I was completely surprised and totally excited about the opportunity. The fact that the final decision-maker called me to interview for the position surely had to mean that I was a shoo-in for the job, right?

Days after my interview, I got curved. Rejected. He and his team chose someone else.

Instead of drowning in the reality that I had lost a great opportunity, I owned my responsibility to control my success, so I went back to my job and continued to give it every ounce of my effort.

But, a few months later, my phone rang again. It was Matt. I had a choice to make. Not just the choice of *Do I even answer the phone call?*, but after hearing him out again, it became a choice of *Do I want to take another shot at getting a management position or do I want to close that door of opportunity for fear of failure and embarrassment once again when the wound wasn't quite healed from the first time?* Ultimately, I realized that I couldn't control Matt's decision as to whether I would get the position or not, but if I didn't step up and own the responsibility for showing up again, then a better opportunity wouldn't even be an option.

After a very similar interview to the previous one, I was offered the management position. Because of that job, I was able to learn from one of the best leaders in my corporate career, Matt. I got my first sweet and sour taste of what it was like to lead people from all generations. I learned to deal effectively with conflict, delegate, and build a team. The lessons I learned and the relationships I built in that role have been absolutely vital to my continued professional success.

But what if I would *not* have gone back to my job and continued to give it my best effort after the first rejection? Would Matt have found out somehow about my declining performance and never have offered me another opportunity? It's quite possible.

What if I would have chosen to shut the door to Matt and any further opportunities because of that first experience with his team? I would not have gotten that position, and remember, that position specifically set in motion a series of events that directly placed me exactly where I wanted to be and where I am today—writing this book for you and helping lead others to fulfill their leadership purpose.

But forget the *what ifs*. Here is what I know: I leveled up and owned it. I could have let my feelings of embarrassment hold me back from taking a shot at an opportunity again. If I had chosen that path, then I would have willingly handed over control of my professional success to Matt after the first rejection from his team, to the company I went back to after the first unsuccessful interview, and even to my emotions (which are oftentimes fleeting and worthless). I am not a Have. I am an Owner. I don't want anyone or anything else controlling my life but me.

So when it comes to your work, realize that you create that breeding ground for success by shifting your mindset to fully own the responsibility for the way you think and act. Haves get curved, and they lay down or give up. Owners get curved and don't choose to sit in doubt or defeat. Instead, Owners choose to go back in and show up every day *even more determined* to perform in a way that continues them on the path to achieving their goals. With an ownership mindset, you predetermine a positive future for yourself.

You will encounter different people, changing situations and opportunities, rejection and uncertainty, etc. The list could go on. The one constant through it all is you. No matter what else happens to you or is going on around you, you can choose to be the one in control of your success. It takes intentionality, but ownership is an option for everyone. And what sets successful people apart is that they always choose to level up and own it.

Now I'll ask you again: Are you a Have or an Owner? If you're a Have, it's time to make the Owner*shift* and take control of your life so that you can crush your goals.

> **With an ownership mindset, you predetermine a positive future for yourself.**

CHAPTER 2

LAY DOWN
THE LAW

If you were breathing in the '90s then you probably remember the infomercial slogan "Set it and forget it!" (If not, YouTube it.) This once-popular slogan makes me think of two things: your future and my grandmother. Ha! Sounds weird, I know. Hear me out.

I lived with my "mamaw" for a few years when I was growing up. Because I was raised without my mother, my mamaw was one of the most special people to me. I loved the nights she would let me squeeze into her twin-size bed with her to watch TV.

Every night, my mamaw would watch two episodes of *Golden Girls*. By the time they were over she would always be fast asleep. That meant the remote was all mine! I don't know why, but the Showtime Ronco Rotisserie & BBQ infomercial with Ron Popeil sucked me in way too many times to count. Over 20 years later, I can still close my eyes and see and hear the overly excited audience yelling, "Set it and forget it!"

If you are not familiar with that infomercial, it was a half-hour TV spot for selling a rotisserie appliance that sat on your countertop. The big selling point was that it made cooking easy…you put the chicken in, then "set it and forget it."

Remember, I told you that slogan makes me think of my grand-mother and *your* future. You've got the grandma part now, but here is where you come in…

Wouldn't it be amazing if life was like that rotisserie oven, where you could just set your goals and forget about it…and in just 30 minutes you'd have everything you ever wanted? Yes, that would be awesome! But it is obvious how ridiculous that approach to life would be, because no one reaches their goals by doing nothing. However, although that approach sounds ridiculous, I still can look around and see many people using it in their own lives and wondering why they aren't getting better results.

Take some time right now to take a hard look at your life. My first question for you is, do you have set, defined goals?

Without concrete goals you risk losing everything because of your lack of direction and acceptance of mediocrity. You have to know—and I am going to tell you right now—that you are created for more than who you have grown to be this far and what you are doing right now. Maybe you know that; maybe you don't. Either way, goal-setting is critical to controlling your future.

My second question (or set of questions) for you is this: Do you feel like nothing really ever changes for the better for you—you're never able to actually get closer to crushing your goals? Is it possible that you are still waiting for the timer to go off and tell you that every-thing is done—that you have finally *made it*? Are you twiddling your thumbs, thinking something else is, or should be, working to make things happen for you?

Success doesn't happen like that.

When it comes to getting the life you want, it is not something you can just think about one time, forget about it, and years later everything just happens to turn out exactly the way you wanted. If that's your approach, or if that has been your approach in the past, you will live and learn quickly that plan doesn't work...but that's why you're here, doing this. You are finally taking control and making things happen for yourself.

So if having goals and wishing and hoping for them to become your reality doesn't work in the real world, what does? What works is making your plan—setting it—and then instead of forgetting it, you revisit it over and over and over again throughout your entire life to make sure that everything you're cooking—ahem, doing—is still working to help you achieve your goals like it should. In our house, we call this "laying down the law."

#LayDownTheLaw

What is the Alyson Van Hooser definition of "law" here?

> **Law:** a clear picture of who you are, what you want, and how you are going to get it.

Let me give you a picture of what the law means in our house...

A typical night in my house right now goes like this... Dinner is over and my husband, Joe, is working late. I'm finishing up dishes, and Alexa is blaring "Baby Shark" for the tenth time on volume level eight. Multitasking from the kitchen, I'm watching as my two-year-old is splashing about a half-inch of his bathwater onto the floor and my five- and seven-year-old kids are acting like mortal enemies, yelling at each other about who will get to wear the Minion costume first.

Whew, just another day in paradise, right? It's time for me to "lay down the law" because this is not how we want life to be going down all the time.

There is something about the mom voice that is so powerful. Suddenly, when I become the perfect mix of drill sergeant and Madea, everyone listens. I yell down the hallway, "Willow, Lincoln, Duke, to the kitchen—now! Line up. I'm about to lay down the law." All three kids freeze. Immediately, everything in the house goes silent—except Alexa, who's still at it: "Grandma shark doo doo…"

"Alexa, off." The kids know what's about to go down. Six little feet pound the hardwood floors as fast as they can go and come straight into the kitchen.

In just a matter of seconds, there they stand in front of me—a perfect picture of the chaos that has been unleashed for the last 30 minutes: one toddler boy dripping wet and the only thing covering anything on his body are the bubbles on his head, one seven-year-old little girl with a face full of my makeup smeared everywhere that it didn't need to be, and the big five-year-old boy with only his underwear on and toy handcuffs around his ankles.

All three kids stand there with their eyes completely focused on me, listening intently without making a move. In full mom voice I say to them, "You all are Van Hoosers. We respect ourselves, we respect each other, and we respect our things. If you all want privileges—like staying up late, playing by yourselves, etc.—you must earn those privileges. You earn them by showing respect."

I bet their young minds are probably wondering, "Uh, Mom, what is respect?" But nevertheless, they get the point! Once all is said and done, their behavior changes significantly and they go back to being the respectful kids I know them to be and earning the privileges they wanted.

#DoItAgain

You know, it is funny looking back to when I was a teenager, because I remember getting out of high school and college and finally going to work with only adults and thinking to myself, "Yes! I will not have to deal with childish behavior anymore!" But what I have found after working with hundreds of adults of all different generations, backgrounds, socioeconomic status, and professional status—and even examining myself—is that there are some things we just never grow out of. Specifically, the need to be reminded of what's really most important to us. That isn't something you can set and forget. You have to lay down the law again and again. It becomes part of your lifestyle— who you are and how you operate.

At our house, we haven't just laid down the law once. It is something we do over and over and over again. Why? Because we know *setting it and forgetting it* doesn't work. If you lay down the law only once, at some point you will get off track—not because you're a failure, but because we are all in a constant battle with what feels good in the moment versus what we want long term.

I am seven years deep into parenthood, and we still lay down the law all the time, over and over again. When things get crazy, we lay down the law. When we're driving in the car on the way to school, we lay down the law. When the kids are scared to try something new, we lay down the law. I remind them who they are, what they have said they want, and what they have to do to get it. Reminding them, making it a part of our daily lives, keeps them on track for what really matters.

Think about it this way: When it comes to my kids or any kids in general, they feel good doing whatever they want, going wild, trashing the house, and yelling at each other until they get what they want.

They like what all of that does *for* them in the moment—the excitement, the freedom, the release. But in the end, they do not like what that does *to* them. They end up losing privileges that they really want. Those lost privileges far outweigh the meager things they were getting in the moment when they were wrapped up in the chaos.

The same is true for adults. Let's say that you are trying to get a promotion at work and in order to get it you have to be there on time, which is really early in the morning. Your alarm goes off in the morning and you know you should get up and get ready, BUT you love what the snooze button does *for* you in the moment—that 30 minutes of extra sleep. However, you end up not liking what that snooze button does *to* you. That extra sleep is great in the moment, but once you have arrived late to work too many times and lost out on that promotion, you discover that all that sleep wasn't really worth it, was it?

Here is my point: It is easy to lose your way when you are shifting to an ownership mindset. If you do not lay down your law and revisit it constantly—choosing to focus on and align your actions with who you are, what you want, and how you're going to get it—then you might have some good moments, but you'll reach the finish line with so many *could've, would've, should'ves.*

This process works. You lay down the law. You speak it out loud. Then you do it again and again and again. When you choose to make this part of your everyday life, then you will harness the power that is already within you so you can truly, finally, fully *own* it!

#LawsNotRules

"Laying down the law"—this process I have been doing for years—didn't get a name until I had kids. I guess I could have chosen a softer expression for my young kids like *rules*, but I wanted them—and I want you—to understand the significance of what is really taking place when you lay down the law.

All of civilization is kept in order by laws. If you break a law, the consequences can be very serious. For instance, you could go to jail, which means your life would temporarily be put on hold. If the offense is bad enough, you could lose your life.

In the same way, you need to have your own set of laws so that you can keep your life in order. Once you have laid it down, do not break it. If you do, you could lose the person, the life, and the dreams you really want.

If you choose not to lay down the law, you risk losing everything worthwhile by going down paths that you never really intended to pursue and that you might not even enjoy. What a waste that would be, and your life is too valuable for that! Make the decision right now to set aside time to lay down the law for yourself so that from this point on you can get to where you want to be without getting off track.

#HowTo

To lay down the law for yourself, you must define:

1. You
2. Your goals
3. How you get there

1. You.

It's time for you to make some decisions. It does not matter who you have been, what you have done, or what other people think about you. This is not where you play defense; this is where you're on offense and you're running out onto the field, proving to yourself and showing everybody what you're all about. This is where you decide who you really are and who you want to be. As an individual, you have the full power to decide this for yourself.

You are defined by your values, your non-negotiables.

There are two reasons you need to define your specific values: *clarity* and *consistency*. When you are clear and consistent, your path to success becomes easier to understand and follow.

Defining your values will give you *clarity* in the daily decision-making process of your life. Operating based on a defined set of values will help you stay on track to reach your short- and long-term goals. Write your values down, and say them out loud. Do this for yourself so that you never have to question what you should do when you come to a crossroads.

> ## This is where you decide who you really are and who you want to be.

You will be tempted to go against your values. For example, if one of your values is respect, you will be tempted to be disrespectful when someone treats you badly at work. But do not break your law. Remember, if you break the law, you could lose the opportunities, the success, the life you really want. You've got goals to crush, so do not give up control of your future by allowing anyone or anything to compromise who you are. Knowing your values, saying them out loud, and reminding yourself of them over and over and over is the key to *consistency*.

2. Your goals.

You must define your goals—literally. You have to know where you want to go and what you want to achieve. If you do not, you will keep living aimlessly. You will continue to wonder when you are going to finally make it, finally be happy, finally take a breath, etc.

The goals you define today do not have to be set in stone forever. I do not think at 19 years old that you have to know exactly what you want to do. I would also say that at 55 you do not have to know exactly what you want to do. Owning your perspective and pinpointing goals is a step of the process that you will have to keep figuring out along the way. *Figuring it out* is a forever game because as you grow, your priorities and desires will change, which means your goals will evolve. That is a good thing! You never have to settle for what you have right now, so keep growing, keep dreaming, keep succeeding. But define your current goals so that you have a clear focus.

As you start figuring out what it is you really want to work toward, always keep your values in mind. Your values define who you are, and the goals you decide on must line up with them. If they do not, eventually you will find yourself torn up from the floor up because your soul isn't thriving in what you have physically manifested in your life.

So, I will ask you this question: What is it that you really want to have or do in this life? There are no wrong answers here; this is your life—so what do you want it to look like? Make time to think about this for a while.

Let me say this to you. It's okay if you're realizing that the path you're on right now is not headed where you really want to be. However—hear me very clearly—it is not okay for you to stay there and never reach your true purpose and potential. I changed career paths five times in seven years before I found what I love, but all along the way I stayed true to who I was, and every move got me closer to where I wanted to be in the end. The same can be true for you. When you determine your destination, then you can successfully navigate the path of your migration.

> **When you determine your destination, then you can successfully navigate the path of your migration.**

3. How you get it.

You have defined who you are and what you want—*boom!* The next part is where the rubber meets the road. How are you actually going to get all those things you want in your life?

This is not where I pump you up; there is where I ask you to make moves to change your life.

For my kids, in the moments when everything is chaotic, their #3—their "how"—is that they need to chill out and show respect to each other and for their things in order to get what they wanted... which was not to get in trouble. However, since you're not a child, it doesn't matter if your mom is standing over you, trying to tell you what to do. This is all you. Your choices. Your decisions.

I do not know your specific goals, so I cannot pinpoint in this book exactly what you need to do to take your professional life to the next level. However, whether you are entry level or executive level, 20 years old or 20 years of professional experience, stay-at-home parent or working parent plus side hustler, I have discovered critical, foundational knowledge you must have, actions you must take, and areas of your life you must *own* if you want to shift the trajectory of your professional life to work in your favor. The rest of this book will guide you through the details of the necessary beliefs, attitudes, and actions you must take to get the most out of your life. When you finish this book, there is no good reason you will not get what you want.

So right now, as you're finishing Chapter 2, wherever you are in the world—reading in your car, in the bath, on the beach, in the school pick-up line, or on your lunch break—TODAY—this is where you put your stake in the ground and start making progress in your life. Know where you stand, know your plan, and do it. Yes, there will be times you will struggle. You will bend, but you will not break. Be strong. Make the choice to keep going. You will get to your desired destination if you choose to own it!

This is all you. Your choices. Your decisions.

You have laid down your law. Every decision you make from this point forward should be made with your law in mind. You will revisit your law over and over again throughout your daily life. As you stay true to your law, you will end up with the result you want. If you don't choose to stay true to your law, you will not achieve your goals. Your life, your work, your choice. Let's do this!

Tool in this chapter: Lay Down the Law

CHAPTER 3

YOU ~~DESERVE~~ EARN IT

Be brutally honest: What do you feel like you deserve? To be heard? A promotion? An easier life? An opportunity? What is it you feel deep down that you truly deserve?

Now tell me this: What happens when you do not get what you think and feel you deserve? You go from sweetheart to sourpuss real quick, right? Most people, instead of pushing through, making a way, and fighting harder, get bitter and give up. Does that attitude help your situation? Not at all.

Let me define *deserve* and *earn* for you:

Deserve: to be worthy of

Earn: to receive as a return for effort

Do you remember *Schoolhouse Rock!* from your elementary school days? "I'm just a bill. Yes, I'm only a bill and I'm sitting here on Capitol Hill." I'm going back to what I learned about the Declaration of Independence from *Schoolhouse Rock!* for this one. "Life, Liberty and the pursuit of Happiness" is what the Declaration of Independence says we all have a right to…what we all deserve. After careful thought and reflection, I totally agree.

The fact is, none of us *deserve* any other opportunity besides life, liberty, and the pursuit of happiness. But hear me carefully: I believe to my core that we ABSOLUTELY can EARN anything we want!

I want to cut through all the noise and junk out there and get down to the heart of what is standing in the way of you crushing your goals. I am shooting you straight because I do not want you to miss the point. I grew up in poverty. I saw firsthand that you will never get to where you want to be if you sit back and wait for other people to make your dreams happen. There were so many generous people who gave me a safe place to live, food, and clothes growing up. I am forever deeply thankful. But, none of them did—and none of them should have—made sure I went to class and got my education, made sure I showed up to work every day and gave it everything I had, made sure that other people gave me professional opportunities, made sure that I learned to communicate well, etc. I had to earn every ounce of my success and claw my way out of where I was to get to where I wanted to be. If you want better, you have to do what it takes to earn it. When you choose to earn it, you are choosing to own it, and when you own it then you can level up and crush your goals.

Deserving it versus owning it is all about your perspective. It's time for you to own your perspective on this and get it right. Choose to see that you have to be willing to go all in and give it every last drop of effort within you to do whatever it takes to earn what you want.

Now, you have to know that even if you do that, you still might not get what you want—but you have to keep pushing. You cannot settle into the idea that you deserve this or are entitled to that and then simply give up when it is not handed to you. If you do that, then you are giving up control of your life and the ability to make sure you reach your goals. You fall back to being a *Have* then! Why would you do that? Don't! Choose to own it from today on!

> **When you choose to earn it, you are choosing to own it.**

#LifesABeach

Joe and I went to Orlando, Florida, over ten years ago and he STILL tells the story of our trip. One might think Joe is still a little… bitter.

The morning of the trip, we left Kentucky before the sun came up. It was early, dark, and cold. Joe was wide awake and ready to go. I was ready to get back to sleep. Joe decided to drive the first part of the trip while I took a short nap.

Well, the nap ended up not being so short. I didn't wake up until we made our first stop. Joe stops the car on road trips *only* when we get down to fumes in the gas tank, so our first stop was in Georgia! Joe drove straight from Kentucky to Georgia while I was passed out in the passenger seat. Joe says that WE got out of the car at the gas station and both went to the restroom. By the time he made it back to the car, I was already back in my reclined seat snoring. So guess what, Joe drove again!

The next time I woke up was when we got to Lake City, Florida. I was READY TO GO! I was so excited to be in Florida. I told Joe, "Pull over, I can drive!" Bitter Bill responded, "Thanks, but there is no point now."

Joe had big plans for us in Florida. He grew up there and wanted to introduce me to all of his old friends, show me where he grew up, and tell me all the stories of who and what shaped him into the person I know today. One of the first places he took me was to his babysitters' house. Joe built them up to be the sweetest elderly couple. I was genuinely excited to meet them, and I was hoping for funny stories about the wild child Joe had been. That visit didn't go quite as expected. It actually ended up looking a lot like the car ride down to Florida.

Joe and I pulled into their house. He said it looked just how he had remembered it. The couple was as sweet as any Southern man and woman could be. Their home was cozy. We sat down on their couches in the living room and started catching up. But I do not remember what happened for the next couple of hours after that! I do remember Joe waking me up, and I realized that I had fallen asleep on their couch for hours—I was so mortified! Joe said the only comment that was made was from the husband, who said, "You really brought a lively one home, didn't ya?"

That trip is funny to look back on, but you have to know why I slept so much. I was not just a lazy bum who wanted to sleep all the time. I was giving everything I had within me to accomplish my goals. I was working to graduate college early so I could get married sooner. During that season of life, I was physically exhausted because of how hard I was pushing to get where I wanted to be. I had packed 19 hours of senior-level college classes into that summer. I had been working 40-plus hours a week to pay for the gas on my commute, books for class, and my wedding that was coming up that winter.

I share the story about the trip not to encourage workaholism or embracing a lifestyle that leads to chronic fatigue, but rather to emphasize that there are going to be times when you're going to be uncomfortable or tired or frustrated, and you're going to have to dig deep to muster up the strength and stamina to be accountable to yourself and the law you've laid down.

That season was not easy. But if I did not put in the work during that time, then I would not have reached my goals. Achieving what you want may never be easy. Life can be a...*beach* sometimes. But when you push yourself to do the hard stuff to get to the good stuff, you will come out physically and mentally stronger. When you earn it, it will be worth it.

#IsItWorthItLetMeEarnIt

Like many people, I worked my way through college. However, unlike many people, I slept in a car to make it happen.

It would have been nice to have had a bed and a bathroom in Murray, Kentucky. Some may say I at least *deserved that*. But that was not an option for me at that time. The law I had laid down for myself was to earn a college degree, and the lack of personal accommodations was not going to stop me.

I got off work at about 10:30 p.m. each night. I would leave Princeton and drive an hour to Murray State University. I knew, recalling my Florida story, that if I went home and sat down, there was a huge possibility that I would fall into a deep sleep. I didn't want to miss my alarm and risk not making it to class on time. Absence was not an option for me if I was going to earn this degree. So, I figured out a plan that worked.

I would get to Murray in the middle of the night and go to the same place—the parking lot of JCPenney. I would park in the spot I felt was the most well lit. I don't remember really being scared about anything or anyone at the time. I mean, I grew up around people who were addicted to drugs and alcohol, so there were sketchy people coming in and out of our house all the time. I grew up around violence, so the idea of fighting someone didn't really scare me much either. I would never seek out danger, but I wasn't necessarily afraid of the possibility. Looking back, I might have done things a bit differently, but at the time I did what I thought was absolutely necessary. I needed to be in class, I needed to learn, and I decided nothing was going to stop me from earning my degree.

So, I would pull into my parking spot and get comfortable. Lock my doors. Set my alarm. Finish my homework or study if I needed to. Then I would lay my seat back. Cover up with my jacket. Turn on Hulu (it was still free in 2009). Then I would drift off to sleep.

The next morning, I would wake up and drive down to CVS. I would change my clothes, brush my teeth, and then head to class.

Life dealt me a less-than-great hand of cards. Yet because of that, did I *deserve* a break?

The reality is, no one gave me a break in class. No one did the work for me. Most importantly—no one should have! I chose to do whatever it took to earn success. I chose to push through the hard stuff even though it was not easy or comfortable. I showed up every day no matter what. I chose to make time to do the work when I could barely keep my eyes open. I *owned* my ability to *earn* success, and you can too!

You can push through when it is uncomfortable, when it is hard, when it is scary. You can make time. You can put in the work and do whatever it takes to earn success. You have just got to level up and own it!

#OffTrack

Soon after I was hired at the bank as the branch manager, I told the CEO that I wanted his job one day. That was my goal at that time, and I made it part of my law.

Because I owned the responsibility of making my goal known to the people who had access to resources that could help me get there, the CEO took on the leadership responsibility of developing me professionally through learning and growth opportunities.

I spent about six months in the branch manager role before I was promoted to project manager. I could not have been any more excited for that project manager role. It was directly in line with the law I laid down for myself professionally. In that new role, I had access to more information and projects than I did before. All of that experience and knowledge gave me a solid understanding and foundation of how banks operate. That was exactly what I needed to stay on track to achieve my goal.

Then, one day the CEO called me into his office and threw me a curveball. He told me he needed me to take the marketing director position in the bank. My initial internal reaction was NO WAY! That was not part of my plan. I did not believe the responsibilities of that role would be beneficial to helping me achieve my goal. I had worked hard to earn the project manager position, and this honestly did not feel fair. So, I said yes.

You might be thinking, "Hold up, you said *yes?*"

I did, for multiple reasons, which I'll elaborate upon in a future book. But for now, I want you to recognize that even when you don't get what you deserve (or feel you deserve) at work, it's crucial to own the result and keep striving to reach your goals.

I had a choice to make then. I could become discouraged and perform at a bare minimum level as the marketing director because I didn't want to do that, or I could shift my thinking and figure out a way to learn something from the experience.

As often is the case, things didn't go the way I felt I deserved, but I ended up learning lessons that continue to be valuable years later. The experience I gained as the marketing director for the bank allowed me to perfect my advertising and marketing skills, which I use today in my own business. The flexibility of that position allowed me to pursue leadership opportunities outside of the banking industry, which helped equip me to train and develop leadership teams as my full-time job now. Finally, having another opportunity to figure out how to make the best of a less-than-ideal situation gave me the mental strength needed to face other challenges in life.

Did I earn that project manager role? Absolutely. Was it fair that it was stripped away from me? It was the best decision for the business, so technically yes, it was fair. Did that make it feel like rainbows and butterflies? No. But ultimately, even if you're thrown off track, you have to choose to dive back in and put in the work to learn and earn your next success.

#LifesNotFair

What do you do when you give it **everything** you've got and you still do not get what you have worked so hard to earn?

You've got to suck it up, buttercup. That is just life.

You can choose to get mad, sit in your bitterness and defeat, and sulk, but you are not doing yourself any favors by doing that. You've got to dust yourself off and keep going with a more focused and determined attitude than ever before. Do not give up—get up. Be savage, not average. Go after it again! Just because it did not work out this time does not mean it will not work out for you next time. Or, even better, maybe it did not work out for a GOOD REASON and you just have not seen it yet. I know that can be hard to deal with in the moment, but you've got to get control of yourself. You've got to own the outcome if you are going to keep moving forward.

No matter what life throws at you, do not let it run you off the path to success and fulfillment. When you own it, you harness the power to rise above and earn any outcome you want.

CHAPTER 4

NO EXCUSES

Most people would not count on someone like me being where I am today because of how I grew up. While I could have fallen under the weight of a million excuses as to why I could never reach my lofty goals, I did not crumble. I am here, killing everything I set my mind to. You can do that too! But how?

You have to stop making excuses. In order to crush your goals, you have to flip the script on your excuses. Start saying...

> I will make time.

> I will make more connections.

> I will earn more money.

> I will learn new information.

> I will do hard things.

Whatever it is that is holding you back, now is the time for you to own it and start doing something about it rather than wasting your life!

I have a very dear friend, Sam Silverstein, who wrote an incredible book titled *No More Excuses*. I highly recommend it to you so that you can dig deep into the excuses you are making and set the tone for your success going forward.

You have to know there is no one magic secret to success, but everyone is better off with a healthy dose of grit. I am a word nerd so let me break down the definition of the word *grit* for you:

> **Grit:** courage and resolve; strength of character

> **Courage:** the ability to do something that one is frightened by

> **Resolve:** the firm decision on a course of action

Now listen up, you were meant for more than mediocre—I mean it! You *should* pursue greater things, choose to level up, and never settle for lackluster living. But that means you have a choice to make right now. When it comes to your goals, are you going to make excuses as to why you can't reach them, or are you going to muster up that grit deep inside you and make it happen no matter what? It is time to step up and own it—no more excuses.

You were meant for more than mediocre.

#FigureItOut

At this point, you've got a good feel for who I am, so you already know that I decided early on that excuses are a waste of time. When you get rid of your excuses, you shift from a worrier to a warrior, defeated to determined, and from wishing for it to doing it. Your success depends on your choice to stop making excuses and make a way.

Maybe it was the fact that as a child I pushed myself to choose exceptional over ease that taught me early on the importance of not making excuses. I grew up without a stove or oven, and rather than settling for PB&J every meal, I learned to cook in the microwave. Not having a stove or an oven could have been an excuse not to cook healthy meals. I knew I wanted something better, so I didn't make excuses; I made a way. As a little girl, I got really good at cooking ground beef in the microwave to make Hamburger Helper for the family. I learned that it is not about your resources; it is about your resourcefulness.

Or maybe it was the embarrassment I felt when my dad called people around our small town and asked them to pay for me to play sports. Do not get me wrong—I am incredibly thankful for the dozens of people who gave to us throughout my childhood. But depending on other people for your own opportunity does not work in the real world. So I decided to depend on me. I made up my mind that if I want something, I will make my own way. I will not succumb to waiting on handouts. I will stand on my own two feet and make a way to accomplish my goals.

Or perhaps it was the fact that as a kid I had to choose between being stuck at home or engaging in taxing exercise in order to get to the places I wanted to go. I lived with my legally blind father, who could not drive. My brother, sister, and I never had a ride to the pool in the summers, so we chose to walk there. We would walk down by the highway and follow it a couple miles until we made it to the pool. The walk was hot, a little scary, very long, and sometimes stinky (there were always dead snakes on the side of the road that had been run over by cars). We could have sat at home all summer wishing we could go to the pool. Instead of making excuses, we chose to make a way...we walked.

Look, whether it was an instinct I have had since birth or something I learned along the way, all I know is that the environment I grew up in reeked with talk and behaviors of excuses as to why we couldn't _____ (fill in the blank with a million different things) because of _____ (name your excuse). But even as a child, if I wanted something badly enough, I would figure out how to make it happen. I have always figured it out. You can too. It's a choice. It's a skill. And you can make different choices; you can learn new skills. *But you have to stop making excuses.*

The thing is, I wrote this book for you so that you can stop wasting time and start living the life you know you are meant to live. I do not want you to have to go through tough situations in order to finally get the fact that if you want something badly enough, YOU have to own the responsibility of figuring out a way to make it happen. Learn from my life and start making your dreams a reality sooner rather than later.

> **You have to own the responsibility of figuring out a way to make your dreams a reality.**

#ChokeThemOut

My middle son has started wrestling, so on occasion our late-night TV shows have changed from documentaries to wrestling and fighting. I have a love-hate relationship with MMA (mixed martial arts). It is brutal. Bloody. Scrappy. It's not the "one-third athleticism, two-thirds acting" type of wrestling I watched growing up. MMA is legit hardcore fighting.

Recently, I watched a championship fight that really stunned me, and I haven't been able to get it out of my mind. This fight was no joke. The woman in control RELENTLESSLY choked out her opponent. She was not going to let up! It was obvious from the time she stepped into the ring that no one…NO ONE…was going to stand in the way of her championship title.

In the very first round, the two fighters got into a position where one had her shoulder completely on the ground and her other shoulder just millimeters off the floor of the ring. It was about to be over. Both women were giving it everything they had, fighting as hard as they could not to lose. One pushing down, the other fighting to get up. The announcers were going nuts: "She'll never get out of this! This is it! It's over!"

But nope, the underdog was scrappy. She made a move that changed everything. Somehow, she wrestled her way out of her opponent's arms, pivoted like lightning around her opponent, wrapped her arms around the woman's neck, and flipped her over to her stomach. BOOM!

The underdog now on top, she took charge and had no shame about her savage game. I could barely watch as she pulled her arms tighter and tighter around her opponent's neck. Her opponent literally could not breathe! Her face was red, veins popping out everywhere. But there was no way the underdog was letting go until her opponent tapped out or passed out. Either way, she was going to make sure she won that championship title no matter what. She was ruthless! She didn't make excuses—she made a way. She got what she wanted! Underdog or not, *she owned it!* She didn't rely on her coaches. She didn't quit when she got tired. She didn't give up when she was just about to fail.

I can never imagine myself getting in a ring and fighting someone, especially choking them out! But I have no problem stepping into the ring every day and choking out excuses that stand in my way of achieving my goals.

The same can be true for you. You can win when you choose to choke out the excuses and act fully on the decision to figure out a way to accomplish your goal.

#WhatsYourExcuse

Life is navigated by your perspective—positive or negative. Whichever you choose is evidenced by your reality right now.

Think about all those goals you wrote down in Chapter 2 when you were laying down your law. When you got to step three, where you started making your game plan, what happened? Did doubt creep in? Did you immediately start making excuses as to why you cannot reach your goals? Did you have thoughts like: *This could never really happen for me. There is really no way for me to do this. I don't know if I have what it takes. I don't have the resources, network, or ability to get this. No one would support me on this. What would they say about me?*

If so, I want you to write these excuses down right now—not the excuses I just named, but the exact ones that came up in your head, in your heart. Now hear me carefully: As you go through this exercise, now is not the time to start putting up walls. Now *is* the time to dig up the real internal and external things that are standing in your way— even if it feels uncomfortable. Excuses rob you of your strength, and you need all the strength you can muster for the experiences you will have to push through to get to the good stuff.

Writing down your doubts, reasons, excuses—whatever you want to call them—is a critical part of owning your outlook and creating a perspective that works *for* you, not *against* you. When you write down your excuses, you turn ideas into physical evidence of what is holding you back. When these excuses become tangible—when you can visualize what exactly is holding you back—then you can easily recognize just how powerless your excuses really are.

Like those MMA fighters, you have to take hold of your enemies— your excuses—and grab them by the neck, squeeze your arms, your heart, and your mind around each one tighter and tighter and tighter until you choke them out one by one. Ultimately, you have to own the responsibility of getting your excuses out of your way!

Your ability to overcome, to persevere, to make it happen boils down to a choice that only you can make. You can choose to make excuses for your lack of success and progress, or you can fight through what is holding you back and blaze a path to your purpose and potential. Choose to make a way…and may this forever be your game changer.

It's time for you to live up to your dreams. Know that no matter what excuse or reason is standing in your way, there is always a way up, out, or around. Do not stop looking for it until you find it.

People and circumstances will change all throughout your life. You are the only constant variable on the path to your success. Do not make your journey harder than it has to be. Recognize where you are making excuses. Write them down. Then choose to own your perspective, level up, and get whatever it is that you really want in life.

> *You are the only constant variable on the path to your success.*

PART 2

OWN YOUR
AWARENESS

In Part One you owned your perspective. Now that you are seeing things clearly, you have to develop a deeper understanding of who you are and the people around you. Bring on Part Two!

No one is completely self-made. So in order for you to be successful, you have to understand how to handle yourself and the people around you. Navigating interpersonal dynamics successfully requires you to own the responsibility of becoming hyperaware of the *who*, *why*, and *how* inside of you and the people around you.

You are the most influential person in your life, so you need to make sure you are aware of what is going on inside yourself and how to manage it all. Understanding yourself will help you stay on track as you level up and own the responsibility to make your own way.

Understanding the nuances of the people you are interacting with will mean that for the rest of your life you will be able to successfully build connections that benefit both you and them. Part Two dives straight into what you need to know and what you need to do.

STEALTH SKILL

You know that feeling when you passed the test—go there for a minute...because you have passed Part One! Most people will not own their perspective. They will fail at making the Owner*shift* because they are more comfortable having "less than best" for themselves. But you are not most people—you are my kind of people...the ones who want more than mediocre and who will end up getting the most they possibly can out of life. How do I know that? Because you are still here digging into this book. Now it's time for Chapter 5.

In Part One we nailed down the choices you had to make for yourself:

1. You are going to take full responsibility for your life.

2. You have defined who you are and what you want.

3. You are going to do what it takes to earn success.

4. You are not going to let anything hold you back.

Now we are moving on to the skills and knowledge you need in order to manage yourself and the people around you in a way that will push you toward your goals. No time to waste...let's go!

#WinnersAdapt

Fully owning your life is a growth process that involves increasing your knowledge and gaining experience living out the ownership lifestyle. In this process, you are going to have to adapt intentionally and correctly to different people and different circumstances at different times. Your success depends on your willingness and ability to adapt effectively.

Adapt: make something suitable for a purpose

Whether we realize it or not, we all have the ability to adapt. How do I know this? Because from the time we are born, we instinctively start changing what we do in order to get what we want. Think about this: We are born with only one real way to communicate—crying. If babies want or need something, they will cry. As they get older and their brain and body develop, they learn to use sounds and gestures to get what they want instead of just crying. Then, we go from a baby to a toddler. We start using words instead of grunts because words are more specific. We discover that we can communicate exactly what we want with words and get it faster. As you can see, we are all born with the ability to adapt so that we win. This skill is already deep within us; we just have to step up and own it if we want to use it for our good.

#SelfAbandoned

I babysat a little girl frequently when I was in middle school. Her parents would go into work really early on Saturday mornings. I would sleep over at their house on Friday and spend Saturday playing with their little girl until her parents came home around lunchtime. One night, when I was 13, my dad told me I was going to go babysit again for them on Friday night. Little did I know, that would be the last time I ever lived with my dad.

I did not hear from him for six months after that night. When I finally did get a call from him, it was not because he wanted me back. It was because the government was forcing me to move in with someone else and he was calling me to ask who I wanted to go with. For the past six months I had lived with the family I babysat for. When my dad didn't show up to get me, they took me in and treated me as their own. We weren't blood related, but they became family. The idea of having to live with someone else I barely knew felt unbearable in the moment. At 13 years old, I had no control over the matter; the government said I had to go.

As this new season of life began, I added to the pain of it all. I was a hurt teenager and I reacted by acting out as any hurt child would do. It took me a while to figure out that I was wrong...that I was hurting myself and making choices that could take me further away from where I really wanted to be. I figured out that I needed to acknowledge my feelings instead of acting on them. If I was going to get where I wanted to be, I needed to shift my focus to learning what made the people around me tick so that I could adapt in a way that would allow me to stay on the path that was going to get me to where I wanted to be.

While that was a difficult season, there were lessons I learned that made me stronger, smarter, more resilient, and more grounded. It solidified my certainty that taking control of your own life is the only way to guarantee your future.

As often happens, that hard season didn't just teach me one lesson; it taught me many...

> *I learned not to give up but to push through. I learned that life is not fair, but you have a chance to flip the script.*

> *I learned that even when you do not get what you feel like you deserve, choose positivity anyway.*

For you to achieve your goals, you have got to level up and own the fact that when things do not go your way, you must adapt in a way that will keep you on track to achieve your goals. You can still make the best of it. You can grow from it. It's your choice. Choose you.

#StayTrue

Something happens to the majority of people somewhere between childhood and puberty. They go to one end of the spectrum or the other. They either give in to every expectation of them and live their life to people-please, or they become so hard-headed and will not adapt at all to anyone else's expectations. Both ends are dangerous. Either way, you risk losing yourself or losing your opportunity. There is an area in between that you need to be aware of and work toward.

If you are someone who believes that you should not have to adapt to meet other people's expectations and everyone should accept and believe in you just as you are—it is likely that you are getting in the way of your own success. If you think that you are not staying true to who you are if you do anything different than what you feel in the moment, you're wrong. That thought process is why most people never reach their goals. So many people remain stuck in a state of arrogance and ignorance that sucks all the momentum out of forward progress in their lives. I hope that is not you, but if it is, you have to do a 180 and start owning your adaptability.

It is critical to deeply understand who you are and what you want to accomplish—that is why we began by laying down the law in Chapter 2. Never deviate from that law. However, if you do not want to be treated a certain way, then there will be times you have to adapt.

Hear me carefully: adapting does not mean you change who you are at your core. It means that when things change, you adjust your attitudes and behaviors to make sure you still win. You should never compromise your integrity or your character. You should never act immorally. But if the expectation aligns with your law, checks the ethics box, and is something you can change, do it!

I've created this Adaptability Matrix to help you see what I mean and use to help you know what to do going forward. If the expectation aligns with the law you laid down in Part 1, the goals you will prioritize on your BGBoard in Chapter 14, and you can adapt, do it! If the expectation doesn't align with your law, BGBoard, and/or is unethical—whether you can adapt or not—don't do it!

It is highly unlikely that you will ever be in the upper left situation…one where something does align perfectly but you are unable to adapt. Why? Because you can change just about everything. You can do just about anything!

Owning your adaptability starts with your mindset shift to ownership. This mindset is critical to your success. Even though it is so integral to the success of Owners and it is an "it" factor in most successful people, most people have a hard time putting their finger on exactly what *it* is. This mindset is simply one of awareness and the willingness to take action.

ADAPTABILITY MATRIX

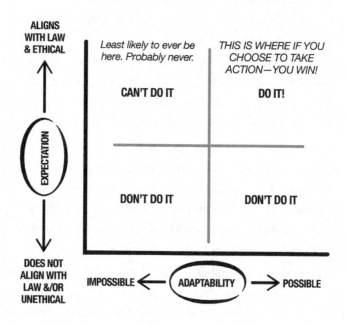

Adapting is the action. Adaptability is a stealth skill. As I said earlier, adapting is something that we are born with, but it is also something that we have to relearn later in life. No doubt, it is a crucial quality that distinguishes the Owners from the Haves. Without this mindset and skill, odds are you will not succeed. That's a bold statement, but I believe it's true both at work and at home. That's exactly why I'm sharing with you the role adaptability can and should play in your success journey, as you will use this skill in almost everything you do going forward—especially with the actions we will cover in Part Three of this book.

Most situations in your life, especially your professional life, will involve other people in one way or another. And the effects of your ability to adapt well to different people will cause things to happen the way you want them to, or not. In order to adapt well, you have to become hyperaware of yourself and the people around you. This means you are choosing to figure out and analyze exactly what you are thinking and feeling, what others are thinking and feeling, and how you can best handle a given person and situation in the moment.

Now, do not misunderstand me here. I am not flirting with the idea of manipulating people. First, manipulation has a negative connotation as if someone is losing. I am talking about a win-win for everyone. Secondly, for further clarification, what I am talking about is taking ownership of how other people treat you. If you want people to move, to make decisions about your future in a way that is positive for you, then you have to adapt the way you interact with them so it is a positive experience for both people.

#RestaurantLife

I waited tables all through college. If you have ever worked at a restaurant, then you know that servers at the right restaurants, getting the right tables, and doing their job well—can make bank! I was living on my own, I needed to make decent money, so I figured out how to make it happen.

The restaurant I worked in was divided up into multiple sections with one waitress assigned to each. Some sections had tables constantly turning over. The tips from those sections were incredible.

Other sections might not see but one or two small tables in an entire shift, and those tips were brutal.

The manager on duty each shift picked who got which sections, and it was never based on seniority, but merit. If you performed well with both customers and co-workers, you earned the better sections.

I had the customer service part of my job down; it came pretty easy for me. But performing well with my co-workers took more focus. Why? Because the two managers were polar opposites. Both of them were incredible in their own way, but they went about managing people differently. Working with these two very different leaders taught me lessons I continued to use all throughout my corporate career—in particular, how to read my audience and adapt quickly.

One manager was a micromanager, and the other was a macromanager. The micromanager wanted to constantly be in the know on what each person was doing. The macromanager was more hands off and only wanted to know if anyone had a problem.

How did I figure that out? I chose to be hyperaware of how each manager handled different situations. I was always watching them and listening to their comments and reactions to different situations.

When I first started working with the micromanager, she would get so aggravated with me. I knew I had to figure out what made her tick because she controlled which section I would get for the day and therefore my earning potential. I started watching how she worked, how she reacted to different situations, and what questions she asked other waitresses. I began realizing that she needed to know what was going on with each waitress at any given moment in order to feel like she was doing her job well. Naturally, I am a pretty independent worker. I do my work without being told, and I do not stand around and waste time. If I finish my job, then I move on to help someone else. I personally did not want to check in with someone all the time.

Now, I understand that some managers would love for their employees to do their work without having to be prodded, but this made my micromanager feel like she was losing control—as if the waitresses could and would get everything done without her. That was scary for her, and I only picked up on it because of paying careful attention to her. If I was going to get what I wanted from her—which was being assigned to the most profitable section in the restaurant—then I had to adapt to her management style. I started discussing with her everything I was doing from beginning to end. And when I finished one task, even though I knew what her answer would be, I would ask her what she wanted me to do next. Did I like working that way? No. But I liked earning more money so I learned to adapt!

Then there was the macromanager. We clicked. She was hands off. I would get my job done and then help others until everything was finished at the end of the night. She would go through the checklist with all the waitresses, trusting that we had done our job if we said we did, and then we all went home. Did all the waitresses work as independently as me? No. But that meant that the macromanager really liked me and that meant that I was getting the best sections.

You're adapting your style, not your heart.

The skill of adapting is beneficial as a baby, as a waitress, in the corporate world from entry level to executive level. It's beneficial in your marriage, in your parenting, etc. You can control your future if you choose to get over yourself and adapt when necessary. You're adapting your style, not your heart. So do not get stuck in an arrogant, ignorant, and defeated place where you *think* staying true to who you are means never changing for anyone else. If you take that approach, you might just get stuck never knowing how good you could have had it if you just would have owned it. Instead, if you choose to be constantly hyperaware of what is really happening in the minds and hearts of yourself and the people around you, then you will be able to adapt the right way every time. When you learn to adapt correctly, you win in the end.

Tool in this chapter: *Adaptability Matrix*

CHAPTER 6

MOTIVATION

One time, when I was in preschool, I went home with a friend from class whose name was Allison. Her mom picked us up from school and had snacks waiting for us at the house when we got there. Maybe that was normal for you growing up, but I do not remember this ever happening at my home as a kid…but I really liked it. *This was what home should feel like.*

Allison had a pool, and she and I could not wait to jump in. We were standing in her bedroom while her mom was digging through her drawer for bathing suits. She handed Allison one, and then she handed me one. Allison immediately scoffed at the fact that I was going to wear one of her bathing suits. I noticed the expression on her mom's face—one where she was smiling so she looked happy, but her eyes were big as if she was saying, "Shut up, Allison." I was only five years old, but I picked up on what was really going on. I was suddenly aware that I was different than Allison, and it stung.

Moments that hurt are opportunities to grow. I have thought about that moment over and over throughout the years. I believe that was the first time that I consciously thought that I needed to become intentional about understanding people. Maybe that initial desire came from the feeling of wanting to understand how other people saw me and why they would or would not want to include me. Regardless of my initial motivation, because of my tough situation growing up, I became a person who watches, listens, and thinks—probably way too deeply—about what and why people are doing and saying what they are. How else was I going to figure out the right decisions to make to get me out of my tough situation? So I watched and I learned. I learned what to do and not to do to be successful. I found the value in understanding what truly motivates people so I could connect with people no matter where I found myself.

We are going to dive into motivation, generations, social classes, and significant events that shape people in order to help you better understand the people around you...maybe even better understand yourself. You have to realize that this is helpful information, but it is just a starting point. Get to know people around you personally—even at work. Get to know them intimately so you can really understand what drives who they are and what they do. Then you'll really know exactly how you need to adapt.

#MotivationTheory

Motivation: the reason or reasons one has for acting or behaving in a particular way

Right now I'm talking about motivation as in why you do what you do, not your level of hype. We will get to that later in the book.

When it comes to understanding people, I am starting with motivation, specifically Maslow's hierarchy of needs, because these needs—regardless of the generation or social class someone is in—drive the decisions they are making at any given moment.

Abraham Maslow published this theory in 1943, and even though it is 75-plus years old, it is still as good today as it was then...hence its timeless popularity.

MASLOW'S HIERARCHY OF NEEDS

Self-Actualization
Achieving Your Full Potential

Esteem
Self-Respect, Self-Esteem, Recognition

Social
Feeling Wanted, Sense of Belonging

Safety
Job Security, Safe Environment

Physiological
Basic Needs: Food, Water, Shelter

Secondary Needs

Primary Needs

The simplest way for me to explain this theory for those who aren't familiar with it is that instinctively, people start trying to satisfy needs at the bottom of the pyramid first. As you satisfy one need, you move up to the next. If you are at the top of the pyramid and something happens that pulls the bottom out from under you, you'll drop back down and work to satisfy that more primary need before moving back up to the top.

Let me give some life to this theory by working our way up the pyramid.

Moments that hurt are opportunities to grow.

Physiological needs: You need food, shelter, and water. If you lack these things, your primary focus will be to get them. Along the same lines, if you do not have a job where you are making enough money to afford a house, food, and water, then you will look for another job because you are trying to solve your physiological needs. You may switch jobs often, not because you are not loyal (which is level 4), but because you are still trying to satisfy level 1. You will sacrifice safety, love and belonging, esteem, and self-actualization in order to make sure your physiological needs are met.

Safety needs: Once you have your physiological needs met, you will look for safety needs to be met. Satisfying your safety needs will look like finding a house that is in a safer neighborhood, or searching for a job where the boss doesn't harass you or where they do not constantly lay people off. In the safety level, you want to make sure your physiological needs are met, but because you're generally able to satisfy them you can now focus on getting to a higher, safer level of those things.

Social needs: Now that you have met your physiological and safety needs, you're moving up to social needs. This is where you find the place where you belong. You find a place to work where people want you there, they value you being part of the team, they include you because they want to. If you do not get that feeling, whether we are talking about your job, your group of friends, your family, your church, etc., you might become disengaged, unhappy, and start looking for other social groups.

Esteem needs: Physiological needs ✔, safety needs ✔, social needs ✔. Now you're moving up to esteem needs. This level is about making moves to grow personally and professionally in a way that earns respect, confidence, and admiration from other people and even yourself. You could start focusing on your own physical appearance to gain higher approval from others and yourself. Maybe now you're going to take on that massive project at work that you know will impress people but also teach you something new. Maybe you're going to go back to school and get another degree. Maybe you are going to do something that reaches beyond you and makes a difference in the world. All of these things are examples of different needs, cognitive and aesthetic, that people in this level are working to satisfy.

Self-actualization needs: Now on to self-actualization (this is where you sing, "Hey, look ma, I made it!"). This is where you seek to reach your absolute full potential. You use your creativity, your spirituality, and you follow your passions. Maybe your job will satisfy these needs for you, or maybe you'll pursue new business adventures. Perhaps you want to fill your soul by exploring other countries…the possibilities are endless. No matter what that looks like for you, self-actualization is where human beings instinctively want to be. It's living your best life.

Maslow's theory is so valuable and insightful into how to interact and make decisions when you are working to truly connect with other people. When you know what needs people are trying to satisfy, then you can adapt your approach to give them what they need but also still get what you want. It's a win-win for your future.

#WhatsGoingOn

If you're like me, after reading the subtitle for this section you probably have that 4 Non Blondes song stuck in your head now. Take that with you into this next example of how a basic knowledge of Maslow's hierarchy of needs helps at work.

Let's say you are hired into a management position and the person that directly supervises you has been in their position for years. You come in with guns blazing, speaking up when you have legit suggestions on better ways to do things, changing procedures in your area, and empowering your people to do more on their own. You are changing things for the better. Everyone should be pumped, right?

It doesn't take long before your supervisor starts acting weird—even hateful at times.

This is where you have to be hyperaware so you can figure out what is going on and adapt to turn things around for the better...for you, for your supervisor, and for the rest of the team. When you are always listening, always looking for clues, you will find them and you will have more clarity as to what is really going on.

Let's stay in the scenario with you and your supervisor...

You two are in a group conversation in the lobby at work and your supervisor makes a quick comment about them working for years to get to where they are, but you come out of college and go straight into almost the same level in the organization as them. Continuing on, the supervisor says that the fact that you were not afraid to speak up and management actually took your suggestions—that caused them to feel like they weren't even needed. Then the supervisor said, "I have to have a job!"

Ding! That's your *aha* moment. *That* was the reason for the rub between you two. Going back to Maslow's theory, your supervisor was afraid that their safety needs weren't going to be met—their job security—which might impact their physiological needs. And honestly, that is a really scary feeling!

As soon as that light bulb goes off, you have to figure out how to adapt. For this situation, you could jump on the opportunity to mend a work relationship! Quickly admit that you do not want their job (let's say that was the case). Then, going forward you would adjust your approach to include them more so they felt like they were a part of the process, not like an outside resource everyone could do without. By doing that, things will change for the better for everyone! (We will talk more about conflict management in Chapter 13.)

The next time you're in a situation with a co-worker, employee, friend, or family member and things are going sideways, take a moment to stop and tap into your knowledge of Maslow's hierarchy of needs. Ask yourself if there could be a deeper issue going on—a need they are trying to satisfy. Then choose to change your approach so you can help meet that need and still get what you want. You will be so much more successful if you start consciously referencing this theory and adjusting your approach. It's a win for them and a win for you.

CHAPTER 7

GENERATIONS

To own your awareness of the people around you, you have to go deeper than just Maslow's hierarchy of needs. Understanding generational differences will help uncover large pieces of what may shape the way some people interact with each other and choose to live their lives. In this chapter, I'll share what I have learned over the years from time spent reading, watching, and studying research on the five generations you may encounter in today's workforce. Our discussion of generations is meant to be a starting point for you when you make initial contact with a person. We will continue to go deeper in the next chapter.

Defining generations is most often done by birth year. However, I believe that defining generations is best done by capturing the events that affected them when they were growing up. I am going to give you the most common names of the generations, estimated birth years, world events that happened in their formative years, and what researchers and generational experts say we may see in them today as far as what they want and how they operate.[2]

---

2 Source of birth year differentiators: https://www.ssa.gov/open/data/EOY
  -Generational-Data.html.

#5Generations

Common Name: Silent Generation, Traditionalists
Born: Generally before 1945

What world events shaped them? World War I, World War II, the Korean War, and the Great Depression.

Most families seriously struggled to find work and even feed their family during the formative years of this generation. Because of those experiences, many became very financially conservative throughout their life. I do want to point out that they are in the last decades of their life and many are benefitting from their fiscal conservatism. Many are often choosing to spend more frivolously and enjoy the rewards from their hard work.

This generation is widely known and respected for their commitment to strong conservative values. They are known for a solid work ethic and loyalty to both their family and their employer. Jobs were not easy to come by when they were younger, so this generation came through the ranks learning not to buck the system because they might not have another employment option. Their perspective in regards to the employee–employer relationship is being fought by many younger people who see it differently today.

It is widely accepted that because many American families in this generation were affected by World War I, World War II, and the Korean War, their perspective on leadership was shaped to prefer a top-down approach. Although this generation does not make up much of the workforce today, right or wrong their influence on leadership still permeates the business world.

Where are they now?

Many traditionalists have retired, but there are still people from this generation holding senior-level positions in the corporate world, as well as re-entering the workforce. They may be coming back to work to earn extra income, they may need something mentally challenging to keep their mind sharp, or they may just want to interact with people more and not be stuck at home.

Whatever the case, this generation is still present and holds decision-making power in your family, your community, and your workplace, so you must think about how you might need to adapt your approach to gain their respect. Because they had to give so much of themselves to their job and their country, they might require you to show them that you too are willing to put in the hours and give more than you have to in order to get the reward. Because they built their career in a time where you never questioned authority, you might have to keep your mouth shut sometimes and just grind it out, even when you don't agree with something. Ultimately, if you show interest in understanding this generation's perspective and choose to adapt as necessary, you will be able to connect with these people regardless of your age.

Common Name: Baby Boomers
Born: Generally between 1946–1964

What world events shaped them? The civil rights movement, space travel, and massive birth rates.

The Civil Rights Act passed in 1964, so as this generation came through the ranks, they've known a work world where discrimination against race, color, religion, sex, and national origin was present but not accepted by the majority. This gave many people the realization of their ability, regardless of the aforementioned factors, to rise up professionally. The civil rights movement, coupled with the moon landing, gave this generation a no-limits view as to what they could accomplish, so they are typically dreamers. But they are also the largest generation, so it is natural that they became pretty competitive because of all the people they had to compete with. They dreamed big, but there were only so many opportunities out there. They learned to work really hard and really smart so they could stand out from the crowd and get what they want.

Where are they now?

Many boomers have worked their way up to high-level positions within companies. They have years of experience that younger people can and should learn from because they have wisdom you cannot read, watch, or buy anywhere else. Because they are nearing retirement age, many of the boomers I know are very willing to invest their time and energy into younger people who will put in the work to learn and get better. They want to make an impact and leave a positive legacy.

Some people in this generation do not like the fact that young people—with half of their own experience—are being promoted into positions equal to theirs. Some of this distaste stems from the fear of not being able to meet some of their needs (see Chapter 6 on Maslow's theory). But it also stems from part of their competitive nature, and it could even come from the fact that they had to put in decades of time at the office in order to get promoted, so the fact that younger generations might not have to...stings.

Many boomers are managing generations younger than them. This can create a disconnect for multiple reasons. For example, I worked for a boomer human resource manager for years. We were at a staff meeting one day, and the HRM brought up the fact that younger employees were rushing out of work as soon as the doors closed at

5:00 P.M. The HRM was so irritated by that and said that was a sign that younger employees were not committed to the company.

This is where communication is key.

The younger employees quickly defended themselves, saying they have family and community commitments that they have to get to as soon as possible after 5:00 P.M. Because the company values included family and community, they were living out the company values by leaving at 5:00 P.M.

That perspective was an eye-opener for the HRM, who did not have little kids at home anymore or hold positions in the community like she used to. Because of that explanation from the younger employees, her perspective and opinion of them did a 180. She no longer thought they were not committed to the company; instead, she saw how they were the epitome of what the company values most.

There is power in knowing the "why" behind what people are doing. There will be times you should not adapt what you do to meet someone else's expectations, but being able to understand where they are coming from and explain your perspective should add clarity and connectivity to ease the situation.

Common Names: Gen X, The Forgotten Generation
Born: Generally between 1965–1980

What world events shaped them? The Watergate scandal, political assassinations, home computers, and the Internet.

Because of there being so much turmoil in the country as they were growing up, researchers say some Gen Xers became very skeptical and cynical of government and leadership in general.

Many of Gen X's parents both worked full time for the first time in history. Because of this, Gen X has been dubbed "latchkey kids," meaning they had a key to their house so they could get in because mom and dad were still working when they got home from school. This meant this generation was responsible for taking care of themselves, which researchers say turned them into very independent workers, thinkers, and entrepreneurs.

This generation grew up with technology becoming an ever-increasing part of their lives. With home computers becoming common and the birth of the Internet, this generation kicked off the tech world we all now live in.

Where are they now?

Many in this generation are in a tough season of life right now. They are caring for their aging parents and for their kids and grandkids who still rely on them. That's a lot of pressure! If they seem on edge at work, maybe you should adapt and cut them a break sometimes.

Some people in this generation may struggle to work well on a team because of the way they were raised by their full-time working parents. Collaborating, for them, might be difficult because they are used to doing things by themselves.

From my own experience, many in Gen X are very open to change as long as you make the benefit very clear.

Like the older two generations, some Gen Xers think young people are lazy and entitled. I've heard it many times as I was entering the workforce and reporting to older generations. You may have to prove yourself time and time again to this generation. However, there are also some Gen X people who are energized by the potential within younger generations and are excited to teach them what they know.

One of my favorite former bosses is a Gen Xer. He was willing to teach and mentor me as far as I wanted to go and grow. He opened doors to opportunities that I would have never had otherwise, and because of those opportunities I have taken on challenges I never would have considered otherwise. I attribute my running for city council at 27 years old to him...and I won that election! None of that would have happened if I would not have picked up on his appetite for building up young people with high potential and made it known to him that I wanted to learn. See, when you focus on learning about other people and figuring out how you should adapt, you can win.

Common Names: Millennials, Gen Y
Born: Generally between 1981–1995

What world events shaped them? Social media, the Great Recession, and education expense increase.

Social media began, exploded, and created a whole new way to interact with people personally and professionally for this generation. Researchers tell us that many millennials tend to prefer text, social media, and digital communication versus personal interactions such as phone calls and in-person conversations.

Researchers tell us that the Great Recession affected many millennials, their parents, and their grandparents. Learning from the experience of the Great Recession and dealing with massive student debt, experts tell us that many millennials are money conscious and are willing to make moves to make sure they are financially stable.

Where are they now?

Thanks to the Center for Generational Kinetics, it is now a widely accepted belief that the millennial generation can be split into two categories: those who are well into adulthood and those who are not, yet.

Experts tell us that millennials are one of the most researched, analyzed, and publicly criticized generations there has ever been. Because of that, and contrary to what pop culture may make you think, many millennials are focused on working hard, looking for a better way to do things, and placing a high importance on making a positive difference with their lives.

Millennials are stepping into high-level leadership positions both in the corporate world and in the entrepreneurial world. Researchers tell us millennials are very open to change because they have experienced many major shifts throughout their entire lives. For example, cable to Hulu, hotels to Airbnb, cassettes to iTunes, encyclopedias to Google. Rapid change has always been a way of life for the millennial generation.

Just as an example, I am a millennial who paid for my own college, got married, had kids, served on the city council, won Young Professional of the Year, all by the age of 27. On the other hand, I know people my age who still have not moved on to the adult stage of life to take care of themselves. This is exactly why you must get to know people individually in order to understand who they are, what makes them tick, and how you should adapt so that you can make the most of your relationship with them.

Common Names: Gen Z, iGen
Born: Generally between 1996–2015

What world events have affected them? Technology and the Great Recession…so far.

This generation is still very young so there is a lot we do not know about them yet. What we do know is that they do not know a world without technology. From the time they were crying in the crib, their Gen X and millennial parents were putting a TV, computer, or phone in front of their face to entertain, educate, and calm them down. As this generation becomes old enough to choose how they interact with people, and how they learn best, the answer for many will be through technology. Whether it be FaceTiming grandma, Snapchatting their friends, Zooming for meetings, YouTubing for DIY solutions, they typically opt for digital exchanges over in-person interactions. For many in this generation, face-to-face communication feels much more difficult than if the communication were to happen through a screen.

Where are they now?

Older Gen Zers are already in the workforce. Younger Gen Zers are still in preschool. What we know about those who have already entered the workforce is that many of them easily adapt to change, similar to millennials. This most likely stems from the rapid change in technology that has affected how they live their life. I'm raising Gen Z kids, and they can talk to the TV to change the channel. Some older generations remember growing up in a time where you had only a few channels and if you wanted to change the channel then you had to get up and turn the dial on the actual television.

When it comes to adapting to Gen Z employees, companies must have updated technology if they want to be attractive workplaces for them. Learning systems need to be updated because Gen Zers are used to increasingly better technology solutions in their personal life and will expect the same at work. Studies are also already showing that Gen Z will want constant feedback from co-workers and leaders. Many believe this stems from social media use. You will want to adapt your schedule and approach to leading them in order to make time to give additional coaching to Gen Z employees.

No one generation is better or worse than the other. We are all different and provide value in different ways. You will likely have to work with people of different generations for your entire life. It is in your best interest to learn as much about them as possible and then figure out how you can adapt accordingly. It is those people who are able to take on a very individualistic approach to interacting with different people who see the most real-world traction.

#ThingsChange

Many industries in today's world are changing. With my experience in the financial industry, let's talk about banking for a moment. With rapid advancement in technology, banks are replacing many of the frontline employees and transactional responsibilities with sophisticated software and equipment. This is just one situation in which understanding generations and adapting to not only industry changes but generational differences will allow you to better lead yourself... and also your team if you are in that position. Here's an example of what I mean...

Decades ago, bank tellers used to keep a ton of cash in their drawer and do everything manually. That is not the case today. You may use only technology when it comes to your banking experience or you may still be interacting with people at your bank, but I am certain there is more technology being used today than ever before.

During my time working in a bank, our tellers started using TCRs (teller cash recyclers). In layman's terms, this machine is used by tellers to process cash transactions. Overall, the TCRs are safer and more efficient than manual teller transactions. This new technology created a totally new way to perform the teller's responsibilities.

This change was not a welcome one for all tellers in the bank. For younger employees, many were excited and jumped right in to make it work. For older employees, many were resistant to and frustrated with the change. Both reactions would be expected based on what researchers and experts tell us about generations in the workforce.

Without addressing the mixed reactions between generations among the tellers, it would have been easy for younger and older employees to become disconnected and frustrated with one another for multiple reasons. However, leadership realized the possibilities and took action. They involved hesitant employees in the decision-making process to ease doubts and confusion. They talked with excited employees about making time to compassionately teach others how to use the machines. Leadership adapted the way they communicated about and implemented the change in processes, and they were successful because of it.

When you understand the people around you, including their generational tendencies, you can more accurately predict issues and opportunities that will allow you to adapt in a way that will make you more successful. But recognizing generational predispositions is only part of the equation. In order to more fully discern what's making people tick, you need to be aware of the role that social class and individual differences play in personality and leadership/employee dynamics. It's to socioeconomic factors that we turn next.

CHAPTER 8

GET ON MY LEVEL

The generations discussion is heavily based on national or worldwide events and statistical majorities. However, regardless of what is going on with *most people* in the world, what happens in a person's home will deeply affect the way they think and act. Our discussion of generations in the last chapter is valuable, but if you are truly going to own your awareness of the people around you, then you have to dig even deeper into a person's individual story.

Within every generation, there are social classes of people. No one class is better or worse than another. Let me say that again in case you were just skimming this book right here: no one person is better or worse than another. The talk of social class is not a discussion on worth. Instead it is a discussion on groups of people who have certain characteristics in common.

Back to social class differences. In general, the thought processes within the majority of each social class further separate groups of people by their perspective on everything from how they talk to what they do. Researchers tell us that each social class thinks and acts differently in multiple ways. If you want to successfully interact with everyone so that you can level up and crush your goals, whether it's at a dinner party, networking event, or at the office, you might learn the best way to adapt by developing an understanding of who is in which class and then adapting accordingly.

At 26 years old, I was chosen to participate in the Leadership Kentucky program. In my own words, Leadership Kentucky is designed to connect leaders throughout Kentucky with the assets and issues facing our state. The purpose is to create a more unified approach to moving Kentucky forward. I was the youngest person in the class, traveling the entire state with university presidents, corporate executives, political leaders, and high-caliber influencers. To say I felt a little out of my league in more ways than one is a massive understatement, but I wanted to be there, I wanted to learn, I wanted to grow. So, I owned it and went all in. I soaked in all the information and wisdom I could from the people teaching the sessions and the people in the seats beside me. Instead of trying to hide in the background, I put myself out there.

The very first day I was there, we discussed differences in social classes as far as how people communicate, interact, and make decisions. From that day forward, I have been obsessed with understanding the differences and commonalities between people in different social classes. I started digging into myself to figure out where I was. I read books that discuss other classes I do not fit into. Let me tell you, I have seen firsthand how this knowledge can help you gain influence, favor, and credibility with different people. This knowledge can be the difference between an awkward conversation and an incredible one, a good decision or a bad one...you get the point, it's important!

Let's explore some of the perspectives that are formed from experiences living in different social classes. Depending on what source you are looking at, there are three to six different classes. I am not a sociologist so I am going to keep it simple and stick with three for the purpose of establishing a foundational understanding in this chapter. Here's what I have learned…

1. Lower Class

> Most likely to be considering their physiological needs when making decisions.

> Know fewer words than the middle and upper classes.

> Talk casually most of the time.

> In regards to building connections, they value how you make them feel.

> Many feel like educational opportunities are out of their reach.

2. Middle Class

> Most likely to be considering their social needs when making decisions.

> Most can talk both casually and formally.

> Value their profession.

> Many will be open to educational opportunities.

3. Upper Class

> Most likely to be considering their esteem and self-actualization needs when making decisions.

> Have a very high vocabulary.

> Talk formally most of the time.

> Value who they know.

> Many will seek out educational opportunities.

You cannot expect people to adapt to you or understand you. You can't control other people, but you can control you. Instead of demanding people understand you, go through life and interact with people in different social classes and focus on building and relying on your knowledge of their values, their preferences, their resources, and their priorities so you will know how to adapt accordingly. When you meet people where they are, then you can truly connect with anybody. When you can connect with anybody, you can access everything. This is just another step forward to connecting all the dots to making your dreams a reality!

> **When you can connect with anybody, you can access everything.**

Let me give you a few examples of ways you might adapt when it comes to social classes:

Example 1: If you are going into a meeting with someone who would likely fit into the upper class, you will want to spend some time learning how to talk in a formal register so you can relate to them and understand them. You might also bring into the conversation any connections you have with people they know because they typically place a high value on who knows whom.

Example 2: If you are getting ready to make a decision that will affect multiple people, it will be wise for you to consider how the effects will be different for those in each social class. For example, I once worked in an organization where the dress code was changed to be stricter. Employees had to wear certain clothes at certain times. The decision-makers could not relate to or understand the true frustrations that many of their employees experienced when the change was announced. The decision-makers likely would have all fallen into the upper class. Those most upset would likely have fallen into the lower class. While the decision to change the dress code did not make a big financial impact on the decision-maker's family, those in the lower class, because they were having to purchase new work clothes, were being forced to choose between things like eating lunch that week or adhering to the new dress code at work. If the decision-makers were more aware of the needs and wants of people in different social classes, then they could make changes that would empower employees to live up to company expectations without sacrificing a person's basic needs.

The differences I mentioned are just the very tip of the iceberg of understanding social class norms and how they can affect how you think and act, so I encourage you to do more research. You have to own the responsibility for learning this information. You have to own the responsibility for adapting and meeting people where they are. Whether you are dealing with your spouse, someone in your extended family, your friends, church, community, or the team you lead at work…your willingness to deeply understand social class norms will add to your ability to truly connect with anybody. When you can break through class barriers, then you open the door to building true connections with the potential to lead to more opportunities for all sides—another win-win scenario.

CHAPTER 9

S.E.E. CLEARLY

Owning your awareness of the people around you is not a one-step process. Bringing together your knowledge of Maslow's theory, generational research, social class insights, and the importance of *individual stories* will give you the best, most well-rounded understanding of why people think and act the way they do.

As you dig into the psyche of people, you will find outliers who don't conform to the generational and motivational information we just talked about. The outliers do not make this information obsolete at all because most of the time, the basic principles apply. However, you have to be able to recognize the outliers. If you do not, you might not be able to truly connect with them.

Outliers will not fit the statistical norm. Why? Because something in their life has happened that shaped them into who they have become, which is different than the majority. Sociologist Morris Massey coined the term *Significant Emotional Events* (S.E.E.). A Significant Emotional Event is one that causes a person to question and even change their values. To create a more influential connection with people, you need to know the stories of the Significant Emotional Events in their lives—good and bad. There is information held within those stories that you will never be able to gather from science or statistics.

I am an outlier in some aspects from the average millennial. Stereotypes and statistics would have you believe that millennials are frugal because they experienced the Great Recession while dealing with massive student debt. While that may be the experience for many millennials, that was not my experience. That significant event in our country did not affect me the way it did many others our age. During the Great Recession (2007–2009), me, my husband, and all our friends were really blessed to have great jobs. That means we did not personally see or feel the negative effects of the Great Recession. (*I am so thankful and do not take that blessing lightly.*) That experience makes me an outlier. I am not frugal because of the Great Recession, but I am mindful about my spending because I grew up with no money and never want to be in that position again. Someone would never know that about me if they did not know my personal story…my personal S.E.E. If someone assumed that I was simply frugal because of the Great Recession, they might miss out on the other values I bring to the table, such as resourcefulness, determination, etc., from growing up with limited means. When you have a deep understanding of the people in your network, then you can fully understand how you can help them and how they can help you.

That example reiterates the point that motivational, generational, and social class information is a good *starting point* for truly understanding yourself and the people around you. The information we discussed in the previous two chapters applies to many people in each generation, but not all.

I fiercely believe that people are shaped more by the experiences they have in their daily lives than what happens in the world as a whole. We are shaped by how we were parented. We are shaped by what we had access to growing up. I am shaped by the fact that my mother left me when I was younger. I am shaped by having had to move money around in my house as a child to feed my family. I am shaped by the teachers who invested their own time, energy, and resources into helping a kid they did not even really know. I am shaped by the people along the way who took me under their wing and became family to me. I am shaped by getting positive results when I have gone all in and chosen to take full responsibility for becoming successful in life.

The same is true for you and everyone else. So while the discussion on motivation, generations, and social classes can be helpful, the fact of the matter is that information is just *part* of someone's story. To truly know the people around you and understand what motivates them and makes them tick, you have to build relationships with them. When you build a relationship established on trust, then the people around you will open up to you and allow you into their lives by sharing very real—sometimes good, sometimes tough—stories of what they have been through that have formed the *why* behind what they do. When you truly understand someone's *why*, then you can make heads or tails of *what* they do. Then, in order to get what you want, you can accurately see how you need to adapt your approach—whether it is your words, your actions, your activities, etc. Those who know the whole story can adapt correctly—and those are the people who truly succeed.

CHAPTER 10

CATCH & CRUSH

I lived with four different families by the time I was 14. The reason that happened was because my mom was never a big part of my life growing up, and my dad was in and out of the picture because of his addiction. When my parents were not around to give me a place to live, I stayed with strangers, friends, and extended family. That might sound really painful to some, but the experiences were not all bad.

Through living with different people, I was able to see and learn that life did not have to be lived the way I knew it at home most of the time. Many of the families I stayed with gave me a blissful taste of what life could be like. I saw that not everyone was operating in constant survival mode. I vividly remember riding the bus home from school many days, staring out the window, wishing the life I was going home to felt like what I had experienced at other people's homes. But the reality was that I was going home to something very different than what I was wishing for. Having parents in and out of my life, moving from house to house, family to family (some good situations, some not so good), takes you through such a roller coaster of emotions, and that can be difficult for a child to deal with. Living and experiencing life with people in a way that was different from what I knew became the

Significant Emotional Events that helped me see the world and what I thought was possible for me in a whole different light.

Growing up in an environment that was oftentimes chaotic and uncertain, I could not wait until the day I turned 18. I literally counted down the days. I believed that once I had the legal power to make my own choices, then I could create the life I wanted. Throughout my childhood, there were times I struggled to deal with my emotions about what was happening, and I did not always make the right choices. Because of that, I was threatened with the possibility of being put into foster care multiple times. That was a place I had heard absolute horror stories about, so I did not want that to happen. It took me getting one last chance *not* to be placed in foster care to realize that I had to level up and take control of my emotions, feelings, and actions. So until I turned 18, I had a choice to make every day: *Was I going to let what was going on in, around, and to me negatively affect how I handled myself? Or, was I going to own my power to take control?*

I wanted a better life, so I chose to own it.

#OwnYourEI

The psychological term *emotional intelligence* means choosing to have "the capacity to be aware of, control, and express one's emotions, and to handle interpersonal relationships judiciously and empathetically."[3] In other words, you have to become hyperaware of what is happening inside of you.

I use the word *hyperaware* a lot throughout this book. The difference between just being casually aware of something and then being

---

3 "Emotional Intelligence," *Lexico*, https://www.lexico.com/en/definition/emotional_intelligence.

extremely or excessively aware of something are two very different approaches. If you are casually aware of something, you might notice it every now and then. If you are hyperaware of something, then your antenna is constantly up and you are paying attention to every aspect of what is going on. So when I say *hyperaware of what is happening inside of me*, I mean I was extremely aware of myself internally and externally. I chose then—and I still choose now—to own my emotional intelligence. That approach has served me very well for decades.

Understanding what is physiologically and psychologically going on inside me has helped me control my actions so that they're not based on emotions, but rather on the law I laid down for myself. When you are in intense moments, the emotions or feelings you experience can seem so big. They can feel overwhelming, even debilitating at times. But when I simplified what was happening down to miniscule neurological synapses, then it seemed crazy for me to let something so small control me.

Let me point out that I am not a doctor of psychology. When you dig really deep into the subject of this chapter from a psychological and physiological standpoint, things can get really complicated…especially when it comes down to differentiating between feelings and emotions. Most people use the words *feelings* and *emotions* interchangeably, but there is a difference between the two. I'm going to go full-on nerd on you—in the best way—for a minute (#noshame). Noted neurologist Antonio R. Damazio said that "for neuroscience, emotions are more or less the complex reactions the body has to certain stimuli. [Emotional reactions] occur automatically and unconsciously."[4] In layman's terms, emotions are how your body wakes your brain up to the fact that something is going on that is affecting you.

---

4 Manuela Lenzen, "Feeling Our Emotions," *Scientific American*, April 1, 2005, https://www.scientificamerican.com/article/feeling-our-emotions/.

Then, after the emotion comes the feelings. Your feelings are shaped by your psychological perspective, which is why you have to make sure you have your perspective set straight. Damazio explains that feelings develop after the emotion when the brain "then processes the signals in neural maps.... Feelings occur when the maps are read and it becomes apparent that emotional changes have been recorded."[5] Again, in layman's terms, your brain has told your psyche that something has happened, and based off your perspective of the situation, you may feel happy, mad, sad, defeated, encouraged, etc.

Emotions are a default automatic physical response to stimuli. Feelings are a default psychological response stemming from our perspective. However, you do not have to act based on your default. You can choose to own your power to act in ways that will get you closer to accomplishing your goals. Ultimately, realizing that emotions and feelings are simply a physiological response to stimuli—a response that does not define who I am in my soul—was a game changer for me. That is what has helped me start mindfully controlling every action I took. I am more intentional about my actions today than I ever have been before. I control my actions and make conscious choices either because of or in spite of my feelings.

Let me pump the brakes for just a minute. I'm guessing that the majority of people reading this book will not be psychologists. While I have done my homework, I'm not a doctor either. So, for the purpose of simplicity and clarity right now, I'm going to own my power to use the word feelings *to encompass both emotions and feelings from this point forward. I share this distinction with you simply to assure you that both feelings and emotions are reactions, not identity traits, and thus are fully within your control to own. Now, back to your regularly scheduled programming...*

---

5 Ibid.

Many of my experiences as a child created feelings of defeat, anxiousness, exhaustion, anger, bitterness, and more, but I had already seen firsthand what giving in to those feelings does to a person—nothing good. So, because I chose to watch, because I chose to focus, because I chose to learn and shift my perspective, I chose to take action that led to a better path than what I had always known.

I have spent time deeply reflecting in order to figure out what process I have been using to increase my emotional intelligence and act in a way that pushes me forward. What I figured out is that I have been *Catching & Crushing* for almost three decades now.

Catching & Crushing means catching your feelings as they immediately occur and then deciding whether you will crush the feeling or use the feeling to crush your goals. When you Catch & Crush, you control every single situation you are in. You will be able to decide to put your stake in the ground and stay on the path that gets you closer to achieving your goals.

When it comes to your life, you will have your own roller coaster of feelings in different situations. You will experience things that, depending on your perspective, will cause you to feel defeat, anxiousness, exhaustion, anger, bitterness, energy, excitement, hopefulness, and more. If you want to successfully navigate your life, you have to get yourself to the point where your very first reaction to your feelings is to consciously say to yourself, "This is how I feel, but this is how I am going to act." Friend, it is time for you to learn and own your power to Catch & Crush.

#CatchTheFeeling

Your reaction to what happens in, around, and to you will determine your life's destination. You are never going to be able to control everything that happens around you or to you, but you can always control your reaction. No matter what is going on, when you choose self-control, you win.

> ## When you choose self-control, you win.

How do you control your reactions to everything that happens? You have to change your perspective to one where you see that everything in your life is ultimately a choice for you to make. You either choose to take one step further away from your goals or one step closer to them. The key to owning it is being aware that you have the power to choose for yourself or against yourself every single day. Owning it means you choose to be your biggest ally. If you are going to achieve your goals and live the life that you want, you have to choose today—and every day going forward—to be hyperaware of your emotions. That is how you own your EI. You have to do this because your emotions can be beneficial for you, but they can also deceive and be detrimental you.

After I had all three of my kids, I struggled with postpartum depression in a really bad way. It was a really dark time in my life. The fact of the matter is that while I felt like I was alone, I was not. I had a wonderful husband, sweet kids, and great family and friends to love and support me. Although I felt like I could not get out of bed, I absolutely physically could. I doubted my ability to be a good mother and wife and thought someone else could do it better. Maybe they could have done it all better, but the reality is that my husband and my kids would not choose anyone else but me. In that season of life, my emotions were deceiving me. They were detrimental to my well-being. I had to take responsibility for owning my emotional intelligence and taking correct and calculated action so I could show up and reach my goals of living out my purpose in my family. If I did not level up and choose to act based on my goals, not my feelings, then I might not be here today in a strong marriage and with three happy, healthy kids to love on.

It is critical that you increase your emotional intelligence and react based off the law you laid down for yourself. That is your clear plan. I said you would need to revisit the law you laid down for yourself over and over—this is exactly what I was talking about.

The next time something happens and you are suddenly overcome with feelings—catch them! What does *catch them* mean? Acknowledge them right then and there as *just* a feeling. Feelings alone should not determine your actions. A well thought-out plan (the law you laid down) should.

When catching your feelings, you can say it in your mind, say it out loud, or write it down: "I am feeling _____." Define it, name it, catch what is going on inside your body. You cannot skip this part. If you want to change your life, take seriously your power to catch your feelings. So, get a journal or open a new page in your Notes app and write down what you are feeling. Make this a habit.

As you start catching your emotions, I do not want you to start developing a negative perspective of who you are. Your feelings do not define you—your actions do. Act based on who you are meant to be, not how the physiological and psychological aspects of your brain work.

When you start acting differently than you feel, does that mean you are being fake? Absolutely not. It means you are making a conscious decision to reach your goals. That is not fake; that is simply what successful people do!

#CrushTheFeeling

Do not let your feelings rob you of your future. The fact is that you do not have to accept your default feelings as the compass for how you live your life. Harnessing the power within you to control your actions regardless of your feelings will be the drive behind your success.

> **Your feelings do not define you— your actions do.**

Do you remember what you wrote when you laid down your law... who you are, what you want, how you are going to get it? Okay, good. As you are catching your feelings in the moment, you need to evaluate them. If what you are feeling is not going to push you closer toward reaching your goals, you have got to crush those feelings. Crushing your feelings is simply a conscious decision not to act on them.

You can crush your feelings however you want. If you have written the feeling down on paper, you could rip out the page, crumple up the paper, burn it, throw it away, whatever! If you captured the feeling in a note on your phone, scribble over it, delete it, whatever! Especially when you first start Catching & Crushing, there is power in materializing externally what you are doing internally. Crushing your feelings is all about taking action to crush your goals.

Eventually, with practice in your daily life, you will not have to write all your feelings down if you do not want to. What will happen is that you will create a new, better default than what you had before. Crushing unhelpful feelings will become your default.

For example: Soon enough, someone will do something that completely rubs you the wrong way. You will feel angry. However, because you have got your perspective in check, because you are stepping up to the plate to own your EI, because you are choosing to own your future, you instantly recognize that you feel mad. In the past, you would have "kept it real" and let them have a piece of your mind. But now, you are Catching & Crushing so you choose not to let their weakness steal your progress. You choose to respond in a way that is even truer to who you are than letting off steam because it honors your character and what you want to achieve. You end up with more credibility and respect than you would have had otherwise. Then and there, my friend, you have owned your power to put yourself one step further toward crushing your goals.

#CrushYourGoals

A couple years ago, I was working in sales. At the first training session for the sales program, they divided us up into teams to play "The Voice." If you are not familiar with the show, there is a huge stage, the lights are down, and one person enters and sings a song to four judges who have their backs turned. If the judges like what they hear, they turn around and you are on their team. If they do not like what they hear, then they just do not turn around.

Each salesperson went in one by one. They did not sing, but instead they had to do a short sales pitch for a small item. When the salesperson entered the room and took the floor, the veteran employees (judges) were sitting at the back of the room with their backs to the salesperson. If they liked the person's pitch, they turned and were on their team for the next year. If they did not like the person's approach… well, unlike the show, someone had to turn because everyone had to be on a team.

My colleagues were going in and out fast. They were all excited and laughing about how well it went and how fun it was.

My turn came. I was not nervous because we had all compared our pitch and were all in line with each other. I walked into the room thinking, *This will be a piece of cake.* The company had fun with the entire game and wanted to make it feel as similar to the show as possible. When I walked into the room, it was dark and there was a light on the stage. The five coaches' backs were turned, and once I got in my place, the clock started ticking and I started selling.

No one turned around at first. I thought they were playing hard to get, so I was still confident for a while. I kept thinking in my head, *I just need to make them laugh…and that is coming!* Well, when I told the joke, they all laughed, but none of them turned around. My confidence started to fade. My last move was to solidify the problem they had and the solution my product had for them. All their heads shook in agreement, as if to say *Good job on that line.* But still, no one turned around. I only had a couple of words left to say when one coach finally turned around. I finished my pitch. I had no idea where I went wrong and why more judges did not turn for me.

At this point, I was just plain embarrassed. The rest of the coaches turned around so they could give me feedback on my pitch. I stood there, I waited, and I listened.

One coach spoke up and said I hit all the points a sales professional should. Another coach voiced his agreement. My coach, the only one who turned around, said that I hit the nail on the head and I did great. He said he waited so long to turn because he only had one spot left on his team and he wanted to make sure I was the one for it. I was so confused by the fact that they said I did everything right but most of them did not turn around. Finally, one coach spoke up. She agreed that I said all the right things, but she cut to the chase and said the hard truth was that I was a female and my Southern accent was a turn-off to her. She said she assumed that was what everyone else felt too, but they were too afraid to say it out loud.

My initial feeling of embarrassment turned to anger. Part of me wanted to quit right then and there. I said to myself that I did not deserve to be treated that way. I started flipping through other job offers I had on the table back home, thinking I could quit and find something better.

However, every situation does not need a matching reaction. I also know that successful people do not make decisions based on their current situation; they make decisions based on where they want to be. I did not need to retaliate and make her feel embarrassed and angry like I was. After a few deep breaths, which gave me time to catch my feelings, I reminded myself of the law I laid down. Quitting is not a part of who I am. Respect is one of my values. I was not willing to compromise on those two things.

So, no, I was not going to let the feeling of embarrassment or anger crush me in the moment. Instead, I chose to crush those feelings. Then, the ultimate clapback—I went on to crush my sales goals over the months that followed. Some of those coaches did not believe in me, but because of my confidence in who I am and my dedication to my law, I was able to use my feeling of determination help me crush my goals.

#IDecide

You decide who is in control. You decide how you will act. You decide what your life will become. Say it with me: I DECIDE.

When you feel angry, jealous, disappointed, anxious, stressed— you make the decision to never compromise who you are because of someone or something else. When you feel excited, determined, focused—you make the decision to use those feelings to push you forward. Every single action you choose should be based on the law you laid down for yourself. Choose to catch the feeling; then choose to crush the feeling and crush your goal.

Emotional intelligence is the soft skill that separates the *Owners* from the *Haves*. Owners create a firm foundation for future success by deciphering and channeling their feelings and also by honing the skill of perceiving others' feelings and reacting accordingly. When you own your feelings, you can own your actions. When you own your actions, you can own your future. Reaching your goals has to be your non-negotiable, so today, make the irrevocable choice to own your emotional intelligence so that you can adapt your actions perfectly to every situation. All it takes for you to get the success you want is for you to level up and own it!

PART 3

OWN YOUR
ACTIONS

Regardless of your age, experience, education, position, or resources, your actions will make or break your success. Part Three of this book is not theory or ideology when it comes to the actions you need to take in order to be successful in your life. Instead, I am serving up practical, tactical action steps everyone should take, but many simply won't.

Now, I want to point out that anybody can do the things we are about to discuss. The reality is, most people who are reaching for bigger goals and coming up short are the people who are not taking these actions.

Why would someone not do what they are supposed to? Well, let me ask you this. You know you should be exercising regularly, eating green vegetables, and using your manners. Why don't you do it? The answer is either because you are not motivated enough to do it or you have lost sight of the priority level of your goals. Again I go back to the chapter on laying down the law. From the moment you put this book down, your law has to remain at the top of your mind. Before you say a word or take a step, you have to make sure the actions you are taking are lining up with who you are and where you want to go if you truly want to crush your goals. When in doubt, reference your law.

No question—the moves you make today will build the momentum you need tomorrow. That momentum is what will carry you through the hard days so that you keep getting closer and closer to where you actually, truly want to be. When you consistently implement the principles in Part Three to take correct, calculated, consistent action, you will easily stand out from your competition and create incredible opportunities for yourself. Let's dig into a handful of actions you need to level up and own it!

CHAPTER 11

BE FOR YOU, NOT AGAINST YOU

This book sets the groundwork for you to be successful. After reading it, you will know what you need to do to crush your goals. But if you are not *able* to do any of what you learn, then you will gain nothing.

You have to expand your mind so that you can think sharper than your competition. You have to practice the skills in this book so that you can perfect them. Your physical and mental health have to be a priority in your life so that you can show up as your best self in every moment. You are going to get to a place where you have high-caliber knowledge, skills, and physical and mental health so that you can take chances, turn heads, and crush goals. To get to that level, though, you have to choose you. CHOOSE. YOU.

I know that as you get older and your responsibilities increase, it is not always easy to *choose you*. Other things become more important... your job, your community, your friends, your family, and so on. But none of them will ever get the best version of you if you do not have your best self to give. When you choose you, it is not selfish. Rather, it is an investment in the people who matter the most to you so that you can give them the very best you have to offer physically, mentally, and emotionally.

#Knowledge

Knowledge unlocks answers to help you get what you want. No one is born with all the knowledge they need. However, everyone can spend their time and energy increasing their knowledge to the level it needs to be at. Most people do not, but you are not most people. When you know more, you can do more, you can be more—all because you understand what is out there for the taking. The thing about knowledge that I love is that anyone can get it and there is no limit on how much you can have!

Knowledge is the solution to every insecurity, every doubt, every fear you have. It was because I learned what life could look like that I started making moves to change my trajectory. It was because I focused on learning more about the people around me that I was able to squash my own insecurities. It was because I learned how to be a better speaker that I decided to get over my fear of public speaking and start doing it for a living. Knowledge is power.

If you learn more about the things you have to manage in your personal life, you can handle them in a way that is better for you and your family. At work, if you increase your knowledge to the expert level, you will earn more opportunities. But both of those successes go away if you do not put in the effort to increase your knowledge. So what do you need to do to increase your knowledge and make sure you are where you need to be?

#MakeTime

First, you have to make time to learn. The choice to make time is a choice for you, not against you.

If your first thought is *I do not have any time to make time*, my response is that we all have the same 24 hours in a day. Very few people choose to manage it well; most do not. You can always make time. Ultimately, it comes down to prioritizing. When you think about the law you laid down for yourself, is what you are spending your time doing each day getting you closer to your top goals or not? See, again, life is just a series of choices, and you get to decide if you reach your goals or not. If you are spending four hours a night binging a series on Netflix, that may be an area in your life to shift so that you use that time for actions that will get you closer to your goal, not further from it.

I heard Dave Hollis make a reference about the idea of treading water on Instagram recently. He was saying that when you tread water, or put things off, take a break, etc., you are not keeping everything the same but actually going backwards. I believe he is right. When you choose to spend your time doing things that are not propelling your journey forward, you are not hitting a pause button; you are hitting the rewind button. You are deciding against yourself, not for yourself. So the next time you have the choice to make a commitment that is not in line with your goals, when you have the choice to veg out on the couch for the weekend or take action that will get you further ahead, make the choice that best serves you and your goals.

#PersonalGoals

No one should know more about your goals than you. You need to know:

> Where have you been?

> Where are you going?

> What are past challenges and future opportunities for you?

> How are you going to get opportunities to reach your goal?

> What resources do you need to reach your goal?

In order to be able to answer all these questions, you have to spend time digging in and learning everything you can about yourself and your goals to make sure you are deciding on what you really want and can see the right path you need to take to make it happen.

Where have you been?

When I started digging back through my life to look at where I had been, what it had taught me, and where I wanted to go, I learned that I was so much more capable of success than I gave myself credit for. Increasing my knowledge through the realization of the relative difficulty of my life fueled my fire to give more of myself to help others.

Where are you going?

When it comes to where you are going, you should have nailed that down in Chapter 2 when you laid down the law. This is where you have to go deeper though. This is where you get very granular and start naming specifics. When I was younger, one of my top goals was to have a family. That is very broad. As I got older, I learned more about what a family should look like, how it should operate, and what each person's responsibility should be. So, as my knowledge increased, so did my goals. I not only wanted a family—I wanted a family with a dependable husband. I wanted a family that I could raise in a safe place. I wanted a family that was centered and grounded in their faith. Do you see what I mean? When you increase your knowledge, you can define your goals more specifically. Then, when you start having to make choices, you already know where you want to go because you have taken the time to increase your knowledge.

What are past challenges and future opportunities for you?

This book owes its creation to the question of past challenges and future opportunities. Because of my past challenges, I now have the opportunity to share lessons I have learned with you in hopes that you will not have to go through similar tough situations and will understand what is needed for you to crush your goals.

How are you going to get opportunities to reach your goal?

You have to make a plan. If you do not make a plan and work the plan, then you are leaving your dreams to chance. Your life, your purpose, is too valuable to leave to chance. This question is critical to crushing your goals because it gives you the framework for a very specific playbook.

> *Your life, your purpose, is too valuable to leave to chance.*

What resources do you need to reach your goal?

You have to fully understand your goal and what all it entails so you can gather up all the resources to make it happen. One of my big goals was to go to college. I knew nothing about what it took to go to college. I had to learn what I needed to make on the ACT and figure out how I was going to pay to take the test. I had to learn how much college costs and how federal aid worked to see if there was a way I could even make it happen for me. I had to learn more about the degrees that were offered and how much the supplies cost for different classes so I knew what was an option for me and what was not. If I did not take time to dig and learn more about the resources I needed to reach my goal, then I would have been unprepared when the time came and could possibly have completely lost out on any opportunity to achieve it.

#ProfessionalGoals

In the chapters ahead, we are going to dig into things you can and should do that will create the firm foundation you need to build on so you can crush your professional goals. However, when I say *increase your knowledge*, I mean that you are going to have to dive head over heels into your specific field.

Owning your ability to increase your knowledge does not mean learning the basics needed to do well in your position at work. That is not owning it; that is just making sure you can keep a job. To fully own it, you have to increase your knowledge to the expert level. Why? Because as opportunities come up, those people in decision-making roles will be looking for the one person who can add the most value to the company and the team. If you want them to think about you for the promotion, be the expert. There is no disadvantage to being the smartest person in the room.

#DreamingInExperience

Owning your knowledge will help you achieve your goals. But owning your knowledge might actually change your goals, too.

After Joe and I put our kids to bed, we love to sit on the couch and dream about all the things we want to do professionally. I know—gag! But he and I really do love to talk business. It is crazy to think back over the years about how our dreams in our professional life have changed…from small to big, from profits to impact.

As you are increasing your knowledge, you have to be careful. You should test everything you see, read, hear, and feel in order to make sure it is truth before you burn it into your brain, etch it onto your heart, or lay it down as your law. With so much misinformation circulating on the Internet, it can sometimes be hard to tell the good from the bad. An example I always use is religion, specifically Christianity. Some believe the Bible is true. Some believe parts of the Bible are true. Some do not believe in the Bible at all. For me, I've had to test everything I hear and do my own homework and prayer to find the truth. It's easy to be deceived in a world where almost anyone can become a thought leader thanks to social media.

Now, let's say that you dig into whatever information or source you've been fed and you find out the information you have been digging into is not true. The process of allowing your brain to think outside the box will give you the ability to think differently, possibly enhance your critical-thinking skills, and potentially allow you to come up with ideas and passions you never would have had otherwise.

For years I have constantly studied the people around me—how they were living their life, what choices they were making, and analyzing the *why* behind it all. This focus opened my mind to different ways of living other than what I was experiencing at home. It is this knowledge that led to my seeing entirely new possibilities for my future. You have probably heard it said before: you do not know what you do not know. If you do not take time to test what you think you know and learn new things, then you could be missing out on incredible options for your life.

#LearningInTheWait

I like things to move fast. There is no point in wasting time when you are trying to get to the good stuff. However, I might not be talking to you right now if I did not put in my time learning and growing at different places throughout my journey. If I would have rushed through some experiences, then I would have missed out on knowledge and opportunities that I never would have gotten otherwise.

You have heard me say this before, but even as a little kid I was constantly watching and learning from other people so I could figure out what I needed to do next. Does this mean that I was patiently waiting for what I wanted because I was enjoying the learning experience? Absolutely not. Waiting is agonizing for me. (I picked that word on purpose—*agonizing: extreme physical or mental suffering!*) I have been through some pretty rough stuff, and I have learned to Catch & Crush my emotions to push through, but even still—learning to calm down and focus on what's going on in the moment, not what is *not* happening right now, has been hard, but necessary to my success. It is necessary to yours too.

Put clearly: Dreaming in experience…learning in the wait… focusing on crushing my goals in the present rather than worrying about what pieces are still missing ended up being the secret to filling in the puzzle and creating the life I envisioned for myself. This right here, helping you through this book, this is one of my dreams. But I could not be here now if I had not been in nine different companies before this stage of my career. I could not talk to you about how to really achieve your dreams if I had not gone through tough times and learned how to achieve mine.

When I took that "temporary" marketing position I did not want at the bank so they could find someone to fill it, it lasted almost three years! Three years of waiting to get my old position back that I loved so much. I made no bones about the fact that I wanted out of that role and back into one that would prepare me to be CEO one day. But looking back I see just how much I learned during that time that I never would have otherwise. And all of that knowledge and experience helps me even to this very day. I am able to market and advertise for my business. I have a high understanding of multiple aspects of the financial industry. I have a thorough knowledge of what customers of all generations want. Sometimes you may not be where you want. You may be in waiting, but that waiting may be what prepares you for the next level. Do not miss out on the learning opportunity you have in your current position. It may help you later. Choose to be present where you are. Make time to stop what you are doing and soak in the value of what you have experienced or learned even today.

What are you doing right now that could be teaching you something to help you reach your next goal? Do not miss your opportunity to get prepared for your future. Choose to increase your knowledge no matter where you are today because you never know how it may benefit you tomorrow.

#Strength

I want you to be living your best life. But listen closely, you will never be able to accomplish all your goals if you are not physically able to go all in and give 100 percent 24/7. You have to take care of your body. To get your best life, you have to be your best self.

I am not a nutritionist or a personal trainer, but I do know what has worked for me and my family. Throughout this book, you have gotten the not-so-subtle hint that I believe in practical strategies to make life work in your favor. So when it comes to taking care of your body, I have simple actions you can take to level up.

> **To get your best life, you have to be your best self.**

#BreakdownToBreakthrough

A mentor told me one time that from his perspective, things really change for people when they turn 30. He was specifically talking about older people taking younger people more seriously when they hit 30, but that was the comment I immediately thought of last year during an accident at a local kickball tournament.

Joe, my husband, was a college baseball player, so he has been in pretty good shape most of his life. After we got married, he and I worked opposite shifts. We had an infant and life was crazy…(*I can now clearly see we were giving ALL the excuses!*) We started living that "brown bag special" life way too much! He and I both were not making healthy choices…the pounds came on fast, and instead of choosing the treadmill and broccoli, we chose the couch and ice cream.

Last summer we were playing in a charity kickball tournament. The game literally had just started. Now that I think about it, Joe may have been the very first person to kick. He kicked the ball into the infield and took off sprinting to first base. When he rounded second…*boom!* He went down. But as fast as he went down, he came right back up.

He started jogging off the field with a limp. I thought his ego was hurt pretty badly. A week later, he was having surgery to repair a completely torn ACL. *So no, Alyson, his ego was not hurt; his leg was!*

My mentor was right…things do change when you hit 30!

Joe has always been in shape, but somewhere between graduating college and turning 30 his body started breaking down and it could not perform at the high level it once did. The breakdown was not drastic or obvious; it was a slow fade. The change was so slow that he did not even realize things were worn out until he tried to do something he thought was easy but left him broken.

It took Joe breaking down physically for our family to realize we had a problem. The symptom of the problem was that Joe was not able to show up and perform at 110 percent—whether that meant making it through a kickball game uninjured, maintaining a high level of focus and clarity at work, or having enough energy to play with our three kids after a long shift. But the actual problem was that he was not taking care of himself physically. My question is, are you?

Joe would completely agree that if he would have taken better care of himself—ate more nutritious food and exercised regularly—then he probably would have had a killer game that day instead of tearing his ACL. But he didn't, and you cannot go back and undo what has been done; you can only move forward and do better.

Since his surgery, we have completely transformed our eating and exercise habits. We started choosing food that would fuel our body instead of simply satisfying us in the moment. We started exercising to build strength and stamina. Joe's asthma has improved, our energy levels have improved, and our entire family's health is better than it has ever been. When you feed your body what it needs, not the junk you think you want, your mind will become more focused and clearer. Both the nutrition and the exercise will give you the stable energy you need to achieve your goals each and every day. Then there is the spin-off benefit of getting one area of your life under control, and that motivates you to move on to bigger things! Now Joe spends his spare time sharing his story and helping people across the country develop healthy habits to change their lives for the better.

Turning the tables back to you, are you eating foods that feed your brain and body so that they can perform at the highest level to help you reach your goals? If not, you are getting in your own way!

I told you that I am not a health-care professional and that I am just speaking from my own family's experience, so in case you think I need legit backup on this, here is what Harvard and Yale have to say:

The benefits of exercise come directly from its ability to reduce insulin resistance, reduce inflammation, and stimulate the release of growth factors—chemicals in the brain that affect the health of brain cells, the growth of new blood vessels in the brain, and even the abundance and survival of new brain cells. Exercise helps memory and thinking through both direct and indirect means. —Heidi Godman, Executive Editor, Harvard Health Letter[6]

---

6 Heidi Godman, "Regular Exercise Changes the Brain to Improve Memory, Thinking Skills," *Harvard Health Letter,* last updated April 5, 2018, http://www .health.harvard.edu/blog/regular-exercise-changes-brain-improve-memory -thinking-skills-201404097110.

The benefits of healthy eating do not stop at simply eating well to feel well. Weight loss, for example, is heavily studied and attributed to an individual's diet. Eating a healthy, balanced diet enables us to feed our brains more energy which is then turned into action, ideas, and constant motion. —The Yale Tribune[7]

So often people are turning to everything else to find a solution to their health issues when much of what we deal with could be solved by proper nutrition and regular exercise. Your eating and exercise habits boil down to a choice…a choice FOR you, or a choice AGAINST you. Do not waste years of your life slowly fading into a breakdown. Own it and make this your breakthrough.

#Spirit

I am not going to take you to church right now, although I could in a heartbeat because I believe it's important. Instead, what I am talking about here when I say *spirit* is your attitude, the core of who you are. Your attitude will predict your future. A positive attitude is a breeding ground for success. A negative attitude suffocates the life out of your potential.

Spirit: the nonphysical part of a person which is the seat of emotions and character

We are all born with our own disposition, either positive or negative. If you are not predisposed to have a positive attitude, own the responsibility to put in the work to change it. It is possible to make the shift from negative to positive through intentional action. Ultimately

---

7 "Eating the Rainbow—The Importance of Maintaining a Healthy Diet," *The Yale Tribune,* last updated November 15, 2018, https://campuspress.yale.edu/tribune/eating-the-rainbow-the-importance-of-maintaining-a-healthy-diet/.

that means that positivity is simply a choice. When you choose to adopt a positive attitude, you are making a choice for yourself, not against yourself.

How do you do that? How do you become a positive person? Well, it is a process. There is no magic pill, overnight solution, or one-and-done item you can check off your to-do list that will instantly transform you. Instead, you become a positive person by making choices every day that focus your mind on positivity.

One of the most popular ways I see people doing this today is by starting their morning off with naming what they are thankful for. I'm instinctively a positive person, but I too have seen this process level up my positivity. When it comes to naming what you are thankful for, you do not have to list every single thing every day—just pick a few. Find very specific things to consciously be thankful for. Write them down or say them out loud to yourself. Maybe you are thankful that you had time to meal prep or that your kid's teacher is so patient. Or maybe you're thankful for your health, thoughtful friends, forgiveness, loyalty, your job, your pastor, mental strength, community, tacos, etc. Find something to be thankful for. By doing this, you are starting your day off focusing your brain on all the good things in your life. If your brain is focused on the good, then it will find more good throughout the rest of your day. Think about it this way: Have you ever gotten a new vehicle—one you never saw anyone else driving around town—only to notice in the next few weeks that you are seeing vehicles exactly like yours all around? That happens because you find what you focus on. Start your day off focusing on the positive so that you can continue to find the good throughout the rest of your day.

You may be reading this and going through a really difficult season. I resonate with that. Focusing on the good may seem almost impossible sometimes, but if you make the choice to do it anyway, it will change your life. If you cannot think of anything else to be thankful for, I want you to stop and look around. There are millions of people across the world who do not have food, shelter, water, or safety. The fact that you even are able to have access to this book (or any book) is a gift in and of itself. You can always find something to be thankful for. Finding it is a choice…a choice to become positive…and positivity is a choice for yourself, not against yourself.

#JustGoWithIt

My dad used to wake me up in the middle of the night to show me things. One night he woke me up shaking my shoulder: "Get up, Alyson! Get up!" He told me to get out of bed and follow him. We crawled on our knees all the way into the kitchen. He kept telling me to be quiet and keep the lights off. I followed him under the kitchen table. With both of us crouched under the table, he whispered, "They are surrounding the house, moving in."

"Who is moving in, Dad?"

"Soldiers!" he said.

We crawled over to the window at the back of the kitchen and stood up just enough to look out. "There they are, Alyson, right at the top of the hill," he said. He turned back around and sat down with his back to the wall, afraid of what was about to happen. I looked through the window as hard as I could for the soldiers. He peeked back up, "Oh no, here they come, here they come, here they come." I did not see anyone out there. That was when I knew…I knew that he was on something that was making him hallucinate. This was not my first rodeo. I had two choices: 1) get mad because I still had to go to school the next day and he was keeping me up, or 2) just go with it and have fun. I made the more positive choice. I could not change the state he was in. If I got mad, he either would not care or would get mad at me. So, why not go along with it and make the best of it. So, I pretended I saw them too. Eventually, *the soldiers passed our house and I could go to bed.*

You see, all of us are going to experience times when things are tough. During these difficult moments, we can choose to see the positive. Positivity leads to success, whereas negativity leads to destruction. Choose to progress, not regress.

#RosetoEffect

The Rosetoans were a small group of people living in Roseto, Pennsylvania, who experienced nearly half the heart attack-related deaths from 1955–1965 as that of the surrounding communities. Scientists had to figure out what was their secret to a longer, healthier life.[8]

The Roseto people smoked cigars with no filter, drank plenty of wine, and cooked with lard. Their diet was not the answer.

The men worked in harsh conditions at slate quarries, where there were constant accidents and illnesses from the industrial work. Their work conditions were not the answer.

Finally, after years of study, researchers came to only one conclusion: the Roseto people lived longer because they surrounded themselves with people who possessed the same character. In their community, their crime rate was zero. Also, there were no applications for public assistance. At the end of the day, the Roseto people chose to

---

8 Information about the Rosetoans comes from B. Egolf et al., "The Roseto Effect: A 50-Year Comparison of Mortality Rates," *American Journal of Public Health*, 82, no. 8, August 1992, 1089–1092. https://www.ncbi.nlm.nih.gov/pmc/articles/PMC1695733/.

be a tight-knit community that supported and took care of each other in good times and bad.

To add even more interest to the story, the Roseto community started allowing the negative influence of other cultures to permeate their way of life. As that happened, the mortality rate began to steadily rise in tandem with the spread of mainstream American culture. Eventually, the Roseto people's mortality rate became the same as the rest of the United States.

When it comes to your ability to choose positivity, think about the community you create around yourself. Intentionally or not, what you surround yourself with will influence you. The places you do business, the friends you invite over to your house, the church you choose, the people you follow and interact with on social media…if they are not feeding you positivity and pushing you closer to your goals, pick new people and places. Make sure who and what you allow in your life align with your values, who you want to become, and where you want to go. Because just like the Roseto people originally did, when you surround yourself with people who feed the good in your life, you could increase your likelihood to truly live—and that is a positive thing any way you look at it.

#Saturday

What you go through does not define you, but it does shape you. Whether it shapes you in a positive or negative way depends on the choice you make.

There was a time when I could not wait for Saturdays. Every once in a while, I would get to go on a trip with my dad. Early on Saturday mornings, my dad would ride with a friend to the methadone clinic about an hour away. A methadone clinic is a place where opioid addicts can go to get methadone (another drug) to help them get off harsher substances. When I said I could not wait for these Saturdays, it was not because I was excited to go to the methadone clinic, but because I was excited to be doing something with my dad. I was willing to put up with the bad stuff so I could get to the good stuff. After leaving the methadone clinic, we would go have breakfast at a restaurant. He was always in a good mood and we got to spend time laughing, talking, and enjoying each other's company. These were rare moments that meant the world to me.

I learned through that experience that sometimes you have to deal with the bad in order to get to the good. I could have completely avoided the bad at all costs. I could have not gone with my dad because I was scared of the methadone clinic. But if I did that, then I never would have been able to enjoy the good part of the morning.

We all have bad things happen in our life. I am sure you could tell me your own stories. But you have to settle it in your spirit that no matter what happens, you will look on the bright side—you will come out on top. You take care of your spirit and you control your future when you choose to focus on the good.

#BeYourChampion

How is *choosing you* really going to work? You have to be your own champion. You cannot depend on anyone else to put your physical, mental, and spiritual health first, so *you* have to. *Choosing you* means you will be able to show up for yourself and for the people you love in the absolute best way possible.

Knowledge. Choose to be a constant learner so when push comes to shove, you know what you need to know to take care of business and take things to the next level.

Strength. Choose to fuel your body and create your own energy so that when life needs more of you, you still have gas in the tank to give.

Spirit. Choose to set your spirit on positivity so that regardless of what stumbling blocks come your way, you can always overcome them and stay on an upward trajectory.

I believe every person on this earth has a purpose—specifically you, because for some reason you are reading this book right now. I do not believe things happen for no reason. I believe we are exposed to things so we can be changed. What are you going to do with what has been put in your path for a reason? It's time for you to own it.

CHAPTER 12

FAIL UP

Do not let Instagram, Snapchat, or some other form of highlight reel fool you. There is not a person out there who has never messed up. And oftentimes, the most successful people have made the most mistakes along the way! How people react to their mistakes is what ultimately separates the unsuccessful masses from the successful few. You have to own your mistakes so that when you mess up—you still go up!

#EntryLevel

Right out of college, I landed a sales position with an international company. From what I read in the description and what we discussed in the interview, I thought it was the perfect entry-level job to kick off my career. Immediately after I got the call saying I was hired, I sat down and wrote an extensive thank-you card to my interviewer.

I wrote:

> *Dear Ben,*
>
> *Thank you so much for your time and consideration throughout the hiring process! I cannot tell you how*

completely optimistic and excited I am to be a part of such
an incredible company. I have no doubt this will be just the
beginning of a long, successful journey for us both. As we
discussed throughout the interview process, I already have a
well-rounded skill set for this entry-level position, but I am
committed to learning, growing, and SUCCESSFULLY
SELLING in order to improve both myself and the
company. I am counting down the days until January! See
you then!

Sincerely,

Alyson Van Hooser

Starting on day one, the onboarding plan was for me to shadow Bill, who was in another territory and held the same position I was taking in my area. I come from a place where the new guy gets the dirty jobs: the freshmen carry the equipment, the new waitress at work has to clean the bathrooms at closing, etc., so on my first day I wasn't surprised at all that we didn't do any of the "good" stuff; we spent the day doing grunt work. I went all in, got my hands dirty, and made a great first impression.

But when I got to days four and five and we were still doing the same thing every day, I had to ask when we were going to get to the "good" part of this job...the things that made me excited about this opportunity. At the end of the week, Bill and I went to lunch together. I asked my new colleague, a ten-plus-year veteran, "When do we get to meet with the decision-makers to start selling?" I wanted to start perfecting my sales skills, but I needed to talk to the business owners in order to do that. Wiping the BBQ sauce from his mouth, he gave me a surprised look and said, "We do not. I mean, maybe a couple times a year we will see them, but mostly we just make sure to do what their contract with us says." What did that mean for me? Ninety-five percent of my job was stocking shelves and making peel-and-stick letter signs. That's it. He confirmed it.

Now, is there anything wrong with stocking shelves and making signs? Absolutely not! The problem was, that wasn't the position I was told I was hired for, and that experience wasn't going to lead anywhere I wanted to go.

With high hopes of professional experience in B2B sales, customer relationship building, budget management, etc., I felt like my bubble had been burst, and I am betting Bill could tell from my facial expression.

"What'd ya think you were going to be doing?" he asked.

As I laid out the position I had talked about with my interviewers, the one I read about in the job description online, it didn't sound similar to what we were doing at all. He was as surprised as I was.

You have to know that I have always had a job since I was old enough to legally work. When I switched jobs, it was because a better opportunity found me, not because I was out actively looking.

At this job, I had a one-hour commute one way, so I had a lot of time to think about what I was going to do. I came to the conclusion that I had made a mistake. There were things I needed to start getting experience in if I was going to escalate my career. I thought this was the perfect starting point. I was wrong. What did I do?

Did I stay in the job because *I am Alyson Van Hooser—I am not a quitter*, or did I own my mistake and start doing something about it that would get me back on track to reach my goals?

After much time, consideration, and late-night discussion with my husband, I decided that I was going to quit this job. It was not fair to the company to continue to train me for a position I would be looking to get out of as soon as possible. It was not good for me to be spending

50-plus hours a week never moving forward in my career or getting closer to my goals from a knowledge and experience standpoint. Quitting wasn't going to feel good, but sometimes reaching your goals is uncomfortable. If you want to get to where you want to be, you have to be willing to crush the embarrassment, crush the anxiety, and crush the guilt so that you can move closer to crushing your goals.

Sometimes reaching your goals is uncomfortable.

I got to work early that next Monday and scheduled an appointment with the hiring manager. During the meeting, I expressed my concerns about the job we discussed versus the job I was shadowing. Admittedly, I had just a glimmer of hope that I would talk with him and he would say there had been a mistake…just maybe I was shadowing the wrong person and position. But no, my perspective of everything was right on target.

I told him I would be giving my two weeks' notice that day. Although I was about to internally combust, he did not seem bothered. He sent me to shadow Bill for the rest of the day.

When I arrived back to the headquarters that evening, he called me into his office before I went home. I walked in. He was sitting, so I sat. He immediately opened his desk drawer, pulled out a card, and started reading it:

> Dear Ben,
>
> Thank you so much for your time and consideration throughout the hiring process! I cannot tell you how completely optimistic and excited I am to be a part of such an incredible company. I have no doubt this will be just the

beginning of a long, successful journey for us both. As we discussed throughout the interview process, I already have a well-rounded skill set for this entry-level position, but I am committed to learning, growing, and SUCCESSFULLY SELLING in order to improve both myself and the company. I am counting down the days until January! See you then!

Sincerely,

Alyson Van Hooser

This was the card I sent him right after I was hired. He read the ENTIRE thing back to me. Can you imagine?! I was humiliated. I think he wanted me to be. I sweated through every single piece of clothing I was wearing. He sat behind his huge desk and stared at me, waiting for me to respond when he finished. I think he thought that I would cave under the pressure and take back my resignation. In fact, he asked me to.

But I was not intimidated by him or his approach. Having to eat my words was pretty bad, but the fact that I had made a mistake in my judgment of the position—that was the worst part. I could have placed the blame on him for multiple reasons, but wasting time and energy on blaming someone else doesn't change anything for the better.

So, I quit that job, and it took me a couple weeks to find a new one. The new job I earned actually was PERFECT. I learned valuable lessons and gained experience that still proves beneficial even today. You see, when you level up and own your mistakes—no matter how hard, how humiliating, how unsure you are of the repercussions—that is the difference from failing and *failing up.*

#FessUpToFailUp

Do not let the fear of messing up keep you from taking massive action toward crushing your goals. Fear is just an excuse—and we don't have time for excuses, right?!

We talked about emotions in the last chapter. Once you realize you have messed up, you are going to have a rush of emotions. You need to stop, take a breath, then Catch & Crush your feelings. It is possible for a mess-up to help you go up. Do not get it twisted though: you should never mess up on purpose for any reason. I am just saying that when you do make a mistake, it is possible to end up better than you were before—if you handle it correctly.

> ## It is possible for a mess-up to help you go up.

In my 20s, I definitely made my fair share of mistakes at work. The thing about it is, if you go back and talk to all my previous supervisors, those mistakes aren't the things they will tell you about me. Most of them do not even remember them—I know because I have asked! But what they do remember is that I consistently handled myself as a professional and they were impressed. You see, even when you mess up, you can still go up.

Your goal should always be to get it right so you do not have to make it right. What I mean is that if you put in the work to not make mistakes, then you will not have to waste time fixing the aftermath. But if you do make a mistake, here is my proven three-step method to help you fail up:

1. Admit

Admit that it was you who made the mistake. I have probably gained more respect from my co-workers *not* by successfully leading massive projects or sharing new ideas that increased profits, but by owning my mistakes. You build trust, break down walls, increase communication, and relieve tension when you step up to the plate and admit you have made a mistake.

I encourage you to take time to prepare for steps two and three thoroughly before you own up. Letting time pass will not make things better, but because you want to show everyone affected that you are someone to be taken seriously, you need to take the time necessary to develop a thorough explanation. However, if there is no time for that in the moment—maybe you are in a meeting when the mistake is realized and the boss wants to know who is responsible right then—that is when you have to pull up your boot straps and own it. And when you do, make it clear that you plan to dig deeper into making things right ASAP.

2. Apologize

You have admitted fault. Now you must apologize. Here is the thing—when you make mistakes at work, it can affect other people: co-workers, subordinates, customers, and even shareholders. Apologizing may be hard for some people, but it is absolutely necessary. Apologizing helps mend the emotional aspect of relationships (e.g., trust and confidence) damaged by your mistake.

Most importantly, your apology must be sincere. You want your apology to speak directly to what is important to the affected party. Your mistake might cost the company money, but if the shareholders are more worried about reputation in this case, then your apology needs to be tailored to match that. Acknowledge how the mistake hurt them and express empathy for that. I say it all the time, but this is just another reason why you must deeply know the people you work with. Your level of understanding of who they are, how they communicate, and what motivates them will affect multiple aspects of your own career.

3. Explain

You have to explain these three questions:

How did you get to the place where you made a mistake?

Were you rushing? Did you not do enough research? Whatever the reason, know it. Own it. Say it. Take time to nail down the root cause of why your mistake happened so you can make sure it doesn't happen again.

How are you going to fix it?

Hopefully your mistake is one that can be fixed. If it cannot, then you have to move on to the next question. If there is a solution, figure it out and do it.

How are you going to make sure it doesn't happen again?

Apologies are worthless if your actions do not change. You have to know the answer to question #1 so you can figure out the answer to question #3. If you continue to make the same mistake over and over, it is no longer a mistake but a choice. It's your future, so choose wisely.

#Unlocked

I had just made it through the training part of my new job at a bank. It was made official when my name was put on the lock-up list. I was in charge of making sure that the bank's vault timer was set, the vault door was locked, and both the front and back doors to the bank were locked when everyone left for the day.

I finished up my work in the office, helped the tellers finish theirs, and I followed them out the door.

I came in the next morning ready to get straight to work. I sat down, turned my computer on, and opened up my e-mail right away. I was curious when I saw the bank president had taken the time to send out an e-mail to the entire bank before the day had even started.

As I read his e-mail, my armpits started sweating, my heart started pounding, and the more I read, the more I thought I was going to throw up!

> *When I arrived at the bank this morning, I was surprised to find that the doors were already open. I went back outside to check and see if someone was already here. They weren't. There were leaves blown all inside the lobby of the bank. I went from surprise to alarm when I was told that the bank vault was left unlocked. So, all night, our bank was left open and the bank vault unlocked. This is completely unacceptable…*

#KillMeNow

I messed up…BIG TIME. Sitting in my office, I had a choice to make. The president didn't know whose responsibility it was to lock up the bank. He didn't ask, either. So what was I to do…do I let it be, or do I own it?

I didn't want him to think it was someone else…that would be horrible for that person. Plus, his e-mail went out to everybody, which meant that all the people who knew it was my responsibility that night were waiting and watching to see what I would do. One of them could even tell him it was me, and I didn't want him to think I was trying to hide it.

As an adult, when people I love lie to me or try to hide the fact that they are not doing what they are supposed to, that's the worst. If they would just own up to their mistakes, be honest with me, then we could start mending what's been damaged. But until there is honesty in our relationships, nothing can begin to go forward. The same is true at work.

So if I make a mistake, I am going to own it. No matter how bad it feels in the moment. And you know what happens when you own it? Let me finish the story…

I REPLIED ALL to the president's e-mail and admitted my mistake. Was it embarrassing? Absolutely. Honestly, I did not know what was going to happen to me. Could I get fired? Possibly. Would everyone think I was an idiot? Possibly.

But I did not lose my job. And months after I sent that reply, I was talking with one of the women who closed everything down with me that night and she surprised me. She was someone who had been in the industry for longer than I had been alive, yet she did not treat me like a careless kid. She said that from the day I owned up to my mistake publicly she had so much respect for me. Before that, she said she saw me as just another entitled kid who lucked into a management position. Because of how I responded to my mistake, she saw my level of integrity and character, and she actually trusted me more and wanted to be on my team. I call that a fail up.

#FailureIsOpportunity

Failing up is not just about gaining respect and trust from the people around you. It's also about the things you learn. Here's an old-school quote for you:

> Failure is the opportunity to begin again more intelligently. —Henry Ford

Henry, you hit the nail on the head with that one!

When I took that job straight out of college and it ended up not being at all what I thought I was getting into, I learned an important lesson. I learned to ask better questions—better questions that would go beyond the surface and pierce through any fluff to get down to the truth. You better believe that when I went in for my next interview, the person on the other side of the table probably left scratching their heads, wondering if they were interviewing me or if I was interviewing them! I even have proof that I learned to ask good questions! When I graduated from the Leadership Caldwell class, I was given the award for "Best Questions." The makeshift trophy with a lightbulb on top still sits on my living room shelf. I am "extra," I know.

After I left the bank unlocked, I realized that there is no shame in setting reminders for everything. I would rather have reminders than miss something important! I started using my Google Calendar like my own personal assistant, and I still do to this day. Maybe setting more alarms and reminders would do you some good too?

Ultimately, it is your choice. It is always your choice. Your past does not have to predetermine your destiny. So the next time you mess up, will you become defeated or determined? If you want to reach your goals once and for all, you better choose the latter. Own your actions!

CHAPTER 13

SALTY OR SUCCESSFUL

Salty (slang): upset, angry, or bitter

Think it doesn't matter what other people think about you?

I would say it does. It matters what they think about you because it affects how they treat you.

People are going to judge you based on your appearance. That's the real world. Do not be salty about it. A salty attitude will not do you any good. And do not become obsessed with pleasing other people; that will just debilitate you. Instead, make the choice to just own it! Choose to get up, get ready, and get dressed so you look like how you want to be treated.

#ItsFunnyBecauseItsTrue

I have made the mistake of not taking my own appearance seriously. I had an eye-opening performance evaluation one year, and ever since I have understood the power that your appearance can have on your success. Again, I do not want you to have to learn the hard way, so learn this lesson from my experience.

I am very fortunate to have had some really great bosses along the way. The story I am about to tell you was not pleasant, but that is not a poor reflection on my boss. It is completely a reflection on me *not* owning it.

When it was time for my annual performance evaluation, I walked up to my boss's corner office. The door was open, and he was sitting in his chair, thumbing through my evaluation. He and I had a great working relationship, so I walked straight in and sat down. I was excited to get started!

I always did great work and tried to find ways to go above and beyond, so I went into it really confident.

Without a lot of small talk, he dove straight into the evaluation, reading off category after category, giving me high marks across the board. Boom!

All of a sudden, he paused. He sat up in his seat and leaned on his desk, crossing his arms. He started turning red, I could see the color crawl up his neck to his face. The whole vibe in the room changed.

"Alyson, in the Appearance category I gave you a 5/10," he said.

He was serious. I could have died right there.

What do you mean 5/10?

He continued, "Alyson, there are days where you come to work looking like you are ready to conquer the world. Then there are days where you come to work looking like the world has conquered you. You're unpredictable. It is all or nothing with you in this category. So, I gave you below average."

My response?

Well, first my mind started flipping through image after image—my own personal rolodex of good and bad days. I had good days where I was in heels and a skirt suit, with my hair fixed and a full face of makeup. Then I had days where I came into work looking like the world *had* conquered me—my hair barely brushed, no makeup on, a wrinkled tunic and leggings. After taking a quick minute to reflect, the difference from day to day was shocking—even to me.

Then, after the mental rolodex was done, I laughed…out loud—we both did! It was only funny because he was so right! There were days when I would be getting all the kids ready before I even started getting myself together, and then somebody throws up and needs another bath, so I have to clean vomit out of the couch before I can do anything for myself! So no, I didn't have time to get ready for work, or else we all would have been late! But then again, I can see a whole lot of excuses wrapped up in that, right? I could have woken up earlier than everybody else and made sure I was fully ready before starting to get everybody else ready. I could have ironed my clothes the night before so I didn't have to worry about that in the morning. See what I mean?

I am so glad my boss was honest with me and that we could both laugh to lighten the moment a little. That little bit of laughter did not take away from the impact of that day, though. That big fat *barely average* score on my evaluation for the effort I put into my appearance…it was the punch in the gut that I needed. Going back to my goals, "barely good enough" was not on my list anywhere! I'm guessing scraping by is not on your list either. I learned a valuable lesson that day that is true for all professionals: your appearance really does affect your success.

#BeAuthentic

Depending on what industry you work in, successful appearance can look like different things. Many businesses used to require professional dress but have now shifted to a more casual look. But do not fall into the trap of believing the pop culture hype and the mainstream media today that is telling you to "do you." Yes, that approach gave rise to thousands of T-shirts and mugs saying things like "namastay in bed" and "messy buns and coffee." But here is what I know: unless you are Post Malone in the entertainment industry, looking and talking like you are lazy is not going to open doors and give you the opportunities you want. Yes, more places are going from business professional to business casual, but no one is going to lazy. If you want to be taken seriously, be perceived as someone who has their act together, earn more respect and credibility, then figure out what you need to look like in order to get what you want, and then make it happen. Not only do you need the skills and abilities to be successful; you also have to look the part.

In a perfect world, it would not matter what you wore. People would see past that and interact with you solely based on who you are as a person. Let me be *very clear*: clothes do not matter at all—they aren't even part of the equation—when it comes to your value as a human being. Clothes are simply a tool to help you reach your goals... and you need every tool you've got!

In every place I have worked, with both men and women of all different ages, there is always drama over what you have to wear or cannot wear. I do not mean little whispers of dress code disapproval either. I mean I have been around enraged adults in meetings going off about how they should be able to wear what they want when they want. It is madness!

Maybe you agree with them. Maybe you're thinking, *Yes, Alyson! What I wear shouldn't matter as long as I get my work done!*

Well, no. Calm down…

Now take those eyes you have just rolled at me and put them in their right place. Just hear me out.

Do not forget what you're doing here—owning the responsibility to make a total shift in the way you think and act so you can finally achieve your goals. Yes, it does stink when someone tries to fit you in a box when it comes to your appearance. But if you want more opportunity, you cannot let anything stand in your way, especially not something as superficial as your appearance.

Now some people might argue that you are not staying true to who you are, that you're being fake, if you start dressing differently. They used to say that to me.

Living with my dad as a child, I remember going shopping and buying new clothes only one time. We would get almost all our clothes from kind and generous people who would drop off hand-me-downs. I am so deeply grateful for those people and their generosity! But when I got to pick out my own outfit, something that I liked and felt good about, I remembered it. I was in fifth grade. My dad bought me a pair of tan velour pants and a red, white, and pink cap-sleeve T-shirt from Walmart for my birthday. I felt like a million bucks! Twenty years later, I still vividly remember Josh, one of my fifth-grade classmates, telling me I looked pretty when I wore that outfit to school the next day.

As I have gotten older, I have worked really hard, and that has afforded me the ability to be able to make different choices. Now I am able to buy my own clothes and dress the way I want or the way I need to for work. I dress differently than how I did growing up. I am much more put together. I live in a small town and see a lot of the people I grew up with—people who grew up in the same environment as me, people whom I dearly love and respect. But I have had a few of my old friends and even family members make comments like, "Who are you trying to be?" The thing is, I am not trying to be anybody but the best version of myself, and I have no shame about that. You should not either.

There may be people who make negative comments about you upping your appearance. They may say you are being fake. My response to that will always be that you will never be more authentic than when you change something about yourself in order to increase your power and potential to crush your goals.

#KeepUpYourEndOfTheDeal

When you agreed to be employed by a company, you signed up for all they stand for—including their image. You and your appearance are a huge part of their image. You are the face of the business to customers every day.

Whether you work at a place that requires professional dress, business casual, or a uniform, there are reasons behind why you are required to dress that way. Do not be ignorant to those reasons. Ignorance can be a huge source of discontentment. Understand why you must dress a certain way, because when you know the reason, you may feel better about living it out every day.

#KnowYourAudience

If you are wondering how you should be dressing at work, go find the dress code in the employee handbook; and if you cannot find it there, then go ask your boss.

Depending on your industry and customer base, your work's acceptable appearance standard may be different from others. I referenced Post Malone earlier—not many people can get away with tattoos all over their face, a messy bun, sweatpants, and Crocs at work. But for the entertainment industry, it can work! If you are employed at a bank or in sales, that look will probably just get you in trouble. Successful people know their audience. They know what their boss, co-workers, customers, fans, and even family and friends need to see in order to treat them a certain way, and they adjust their appearance accordingly.

I remember how my co-workers treated me when I was put together versus looking like I was barely holding it together.

If I got up and made the effort to look like a professional, not only did I feel better about myself and had more motivation to kill it at work, but it seemed like everyone I came in contact with was more positive, upbeat, and open to conversation at work.

On the other hand, I also remember lots of "Are you feeling okay?" questions on the days where I didn't put much effort into my appearance. Looking back, I cannot help but wonder how many opportunities I missed out on because someone thought I didn't feel well or was too tired to take on a new project or learn a new skill.

Because my appearance was unpredictable and less than what my boss expected half the time, how did that affect his perception of the actual work I did? Did he think that I approached my work in the same way as my appearance...barely average, or inconsistent? Were there conversations around the board table about promoting me, but he shot them down because he subconsciously wondered if I had the discipline to take on more responsibility if I did not have the discipline to show up professionally?

What about you? How many opportunities have you likely missed out on because you have just been out there "doing you" or making excuses as to why you do not have it together on a given day?

There was an interesting study conducted by Hajo Adam and Adam Galinsky, published in 2012 by the American Psychology Association, that showed the connection between what you wear and how you feel and act. They introduced the term "enclothed cognition." In simple terms, their conclusion was that depending on what you are wearing and how you feel about it, that will affect how you perform. So, if you feel like what you are wearing is powerful, exudes confidence, and makes you look smart and accomplished, then *enclothed cognition* would lead me to the conclusion that you will perform powerfully, confidently, intelligently, and become accomplished because of it.

Yes, the clothes you wear are important, but the thing you do not want to miss about this is the importance of owning your entire appearance, meaning all aspects of anything that someone can observe about you.

#Appearance360

Your in-person appearance is not just your clothes, hair, and makeup. It's how you walk, how you talk...how you smell for goodness' sake.

But times have changed. You do not have to just manage your in-person appearance; you have an online appearance you have to manage too.

#FaceToFace

When you walk in a room, whether it be a living room or a board-room, before you say a word people consciously or subconsciously are forming opinions about you. Remember why this matters—because it affects how they treat you. You can control the amount of respect, credibility, and opportunity people are willing to give you by the way you carry yourself.

If you show up looking like a hot mess, do not be surprised when you are treated like a hot mess. If someone else is showing up looking like they are ready to kill it every day, do not be salty when they start getting more opportunities than you. If you want it, own it!

#ThinkActLookLikeAPro

Professionalism is a choice to perform at the highest level. If you want success, you need to think, act, and look like a pro.

1. Think like a leader—know what is expected of you.

Dress for your audience. Look like the person your company and your customers want to see and know.

Know your company dress code and make sure you follow it to a T. Find reasons to go above and beyond, but stay within the guidelines. Never find ways to push the boundaries so you can squeeze something in and hope it is overlooked. That approach will be noticed, and it will hurt you. It is widely acceptable to be overdressed but never acceptable to be underdressed. You may work in a company where casual dress is allowed and even preferred—go for it. Or you may work in a place where business casual is accepted, but professional dress is preferred. If that's the case, suit up so you can stand out!

> ## Professionalism is a choice to perform at the highest level.

2. Think like a leader—no excuses.

How many of you do not have the money to buy the things you think you need so you can appear a certain way going forward? Well, remember what we discussed in Chapter 4...do not make excuses as to why you cannot reach your goals—make a way. So find a way to get the things you need.

There is no shame in hand-me-downs. There is no shame in thrifting. There is no shame in wearing the same clothes every day. I had only one pair of black work pants for my all-black restaurant uniform for years. Unless your goal is to be a fashion blogger, do not worry about having the latest and greatest. Spend your time focusing on making the best of what you have.

If you consistently put in the effort to be put together, decision-makers will notice your discipline. It may be that they do not recognize you differently for what you *are* doing, but instead they recognize you for what you *are not* doing. If you are always in line with the expectation, then they do not have to worry about your becoming a distraction or wasting their time dealing with your dress code issues. Where that becomes really important is when a leader has an opportunity to give, and it is between you and someone else. Of course, they will pick the person who causes the least amount of problems. So you will reap the benefits of dressing to their expectations. It's possible that those benefits could even be promotions that lead to an increased salary that allows you to buy those clothes in which you picture yourself.

Again, clothes are just a tool. But this tool can help open doors. Dress the part, no excuses.

3. Act like a leader—wake up early.

Not having enough time to get ready should never be a reason you are not showing up to work, prepared and ready to go. There is always enough time if you make enough time.

Wake up early. Make sure you have plenty of time to fix your hair, shower, wash your face, iron any wrinkles in your clothes, and still be EARLY for work. Do not walk in at the last minute. Even if you look amazing, your lack of punctuality will overshadow that.

Women, consistency is key when it comes to makeup. I learned that the hard way. Remember…5/10. If you wear a full face of makeup all the time, do that all the time. If you wear a full face of makeup one day and nothing the next—it is shocking to people. I can say that; I am a woman too (insert the panda bear mascara meme). It stinks, I know, but do not give people a reason to ask or wonder if you feel okay today. Make people say, "Dang, she's got it together every day!" Make them feel confident in your ability to take care of the things that need to be taken care of so they will trust that you can handle the next big opportunity. Side note: I am not saying you have to wear makeup. I am saying whatever you do, do it every day. Be consistent.

Back to waking up early…

Are you a night owl like me? I am not a morning person. I would rather stay up all night and start getting ready at 4:30 A.M. than go to bed at 8:30 P.M. and get up at 4:30 A.M. But sleep is necessary to make your brain work, so go to bed early and get up early.

I now wake up at 4:30 A.M. most mornings. I have to because I have goals and there are things I need to do! There is nothing magic about 4:30 A.M. You need to find out what the best time is for you to start your day. Whatever time that is, plan for the amount of time you need to get ready. Take eating, exercising, dealing with issues that may come up, the time it takes to get ready, and your commute time all into consideration when deciding what time you will start waking up in order to arrive at work 15 minutes early—yes, early!

For me, the act of actually getting out of bed is the hardest part of waking up early. Once I am up and ready, as long as I went to bed early enough the night before, I do not feel overtired. If I feel tired, it is because my nutrition and exercise are off.

There are some really innovative things you can do to make yourself get up early. You can get alarm clocks that roll around on the floor so you actually have to get up to turn them off. You can set your phone alarm in another room so that you are forced to get out of bed to silence it. The thing I started doing and would suggest for you is when the alarm goes off, stand up immediately. Like a soldier after the morning trumpet wake-up call, stand straight up and start walking. You may not like it. You may hate it. I did not like it at all. Sometimes I still hate it. But you are up, and eventually your body will learn to wake up on its own at that time and you will stop hating it.

Waking up early enough to get yourself together is a choice. Even if it is hard, make decisions that work for you, not against you.

4. Look like a leader—do not wear wrinkled clothes.

No matter what industry or business you are in, it is never acceptable for you to have wrinkled clothes. As a former supervisor, I would hands down take someone wearing the exact same thing every day that is clean and ironed over someone looking sloppy with the latest and greatest fashion trends.

No matter how nice your clothes are, if they are wrinkled, you will look sloppy. Buy an iron and use it—no excuses. This is a simple, small detail that makes a big difference in your whole appearance.

I am sure there are people out there looking at someone with wrinkled clothes, thinking, *They didn't make time to iron their clothes. I guess they just do not care. If they do not care about how they look at their job, maybe they do not really care about their job either.* I wouldn't want someone who holds the decision-making power within my company ever thinking there is a possibility I do not care about my job.

Again, this is small stuff. It can seem insignificant in the big picture of things, but we are knocking out every little detail of obstacles that can get in the way of you accomplishing your goals. So, own this. Make sure your clothes are not wrinkled.

5. Act like a leader—walk and talk like a professional.

You communicate verbally and nonverbally. Both affect how other people see you. Again, that is only relevant because it affects how they treat you. And if reaching your goals requires doors to be opened to other people, places, and/or information, then their opinion of you matters.

When it comes to your nonverbals—how you walk, how you sit, the expression on your face—you must be hyperaware of these things. Amy Cuddy is a social psychologist and Harvard lecturer. You might have seen her TED Talk on body language that has over 16 million views on YouTube. Cuddy says you can change how you feel about yourself and what other people think about you through your body language.

From the moment you pull into the parking lot at work, be thoughtful about what your body language is communicating. Walk in like you have got somewhere to be! Do not slump around work all day like Eeyore—walk with confidence and purpose. When you're sitting in a meeting, do not slouch. Sit up, lean in—be interested and attentive. Then there is your face. Have you seen all the memes about "resting b#$@! face"? They are funny, but in reality, you have to control your face. Be aware of your facial expressions. Smile. Look positive and approachable. Nobody wants to do business with someone who looks unhappy and closed off.

Successful people also set themselves apart by the way they talk. Your tone of voice, pacing, volume, word choice, and subject matter all make a difference! Every word you speak is an opportunity for you to gain or lose credibility and respect, so choose your words wisely.

With regard to the content of your speech, it is always better to err on the side of caution...

Do not tell dirty jokes. You risk losing respect from people. Find other ways to be funny.

Do not use profanity. You risk losing credibility. Research other words that will get your point across.

Do not gossip. This will create distrust and negativity. Successful people do not swim around in that kind of environment. They do not even dip their toe in.

Do not complain. Use your words to stir up positivity and excellence in the organization that will fuel you and everyone else to become better.

Talk like the professional you want others to see you as.

#OnlineAppearance

What you share, say, like, and follow on social media is being watched and is being held *for* you or *against* you. So what do your posts say about who you are, your work ethic, and what it would be like to have you on the team? Are you helping or hurting yourself?

Most people use their personal social media to interact with people they know. Most people think it is totally acceptable to post whatever they want whenever they want because it is **their** (Facebook, Instagram, Snapchat, Twitter, YouTube, etc.) account, right? Do not be most people! Yes, it is your personal account, but are you aware you could actually be killing your own career by what you're doing on social media? Here are three examples of what I mean:

1. Your "private" setting doesn't mean you're completely hidden.

Are you thinking about what your boss, co-workers, or customers will think about what you're posting BEFORE you put it out there for the world to see?

Most people think that because their profile is set to "private" that only the people they want to see their information will see it. That is just not the case.

I have been on the employer's side of the table, where we were trying to get a feel for who someone really is before bringing them in for an interview. Just like "six degrees of Kevin Bacon," employers will find *someone somewhere* they know who is connected with you on social so they can check out your profile.

Take your social media seriously and do not post anything that would shift how others think about you in a negative way.

2. Do not rant on social media.

I have sat around a computer with leaders and looked at applicants' social media profiles. How do you think the conversation goes when decision-makers see rants about poor food service, your irritation with bad drivers, and your hatred of Mondays from people who are wanting a job or promotion?

I can tell you, it is not good news for the applicant or the employee.

When decision-makers read those ranting posts, it leaves them with questions like, "How much self-discipline does this person have?" or "I wonder if they can control their mouth?" They begin to think, "It sounds like they have a bad attitude." Ultimately, if you rant on social media, you risk losing opportunities.

Remember, your employer, your co-workers, your customers—they are your audience, and they are watching. Handle yourself like a professional on social media. Do not miss out on long-term opportunity simply because you want a short-term emotional release through ranting.

3. Do not connect and then block people.

If you connect on social media with everyone at work on your first day, then a few months later you block everyone, you are going to raise some red flags with those people.

Making this mistake causes thoughts to creep into your co-workers' minds like, "What are they trying to hide?" It can make people wonder if you are doing something you're not supposed to do or if you are looking for another job. I know because I have seen and heard it happen! Do not give people a reason to doubt you.

I have had so many conversations about giving someone a job in the corporate world, appointing someone to a position of authority within local government, offering someone an opportunity for service at church, and the person's social media activity always—not some-times—always comes into the conversation.

Both in person and online, choose to show up 24/7 as the person to whom people will want to give opportunities. Do not let anything stand in your way of achieving your goals.

When it comes to your appearance, do what you have to do so that you can do what you want to do. Owning it in this area of your life is about shifting your mindset to understanding that the most authentic self-expression is the one that enables you to crush your goals. That's why it's crucial that you use all aspects of your appearance to get what you want out of life. You have many tools that can affect the way other people see and perceive you. Use every tool intentionally. Level up and own it!

The most authentic self-expression is the one that enables you to crush your goals.

CHAPTER 14

GET IT TOGETHER

Question: *True* or *False*—
good things come to those who hustle?
Answer: It depends.

Maybe you are a hustler—someone who grinds it out sun up to sun down—and you come home completely exhausted. But what if all your hustle was leading to nothing? What if you killed yourself working but still did not accomplish your goals because at the end of the day, you were working on the wrong things? If you are going to get to where you want to go, you've got to take a long, hard look at what you are actually doing, or not doing, every single day.

We all have the same 24 hours in a day. Some people crush their goals in those 24 hours; some do not. The difference comes down to your willingness to prioritize. Time management is a choice. If you want to own your future and crush your goals, you have to choose to take the actions that will give you the best chance at getting what you want.

#WorkDontWish

Figuring out what your goals are—and, in so doing, laying down your law—is critical to your overall success, but if that is as far as you get, then that is as far as you will ever get. You will achieve only what you work for, not what you merely wish for.

I was basically on my own growing up. I got ready for school in the morning, did my homework the night before, made sure I had a ride to and from practice, squeezed in time for my friends down the street—all of it, by hook or by crook, I made sure I got it done. From that experience, I learned that I could not always do what felt like the most fun or the easiest option in the moment. I had to prioritize if I was going to be able to accomplish the things I really wanted—my big goals. I did not spend time *managing* my time as a little kid; my instincts took over. But as my goals became more difficult to reach, I had to make the time to plan my time. I still do that today every day.

Most people who feel like they cannot get everything done that they need to are spending time doing things throughout their day that do not get them any closer to what they really want—their goals. The key to reaching your goals is taking the *right* action. Choose to take action today that will give you more time to spend working toward your goals.

Get back more time in your day when you do things like:

> Stop watching TV and go check something off your list.

> Pack your lunch and eat in the office rather than going out for an hour.

> Meal prep ahead of time so you do not have to spend time cooking every night.

> Make important phone calls during your drive to work instead of cranking up your music and chilling.

> Wake up earlier.

> Skip the Sunday afternoon nap.

> Make your kids help with chores.

> Work while you wait at the doctor's office, hair salon, etc.

> Ask someone for help. Hire them or ask for a favor and repay them later. Get someone to manage your website, watch your kids, clean your house, etc., so you can spend focused time on goal-reaching.

> Order your groceries online so you don't get stuck talking to people in the store.

> Use 2-in-1 shampoo/conditioner…I am kidding; that is not worth the sacrifice.

But once you have cut down on all your wasted time, you have to make sure that what you are doing is ONLY the things that put you closer to achieving your goals. Don't fall into the trap of getting distracted by projects or tasks that don't align with your ultimate objectives.

You will achieve only what you work for, not what you merely wish for.

#BGBoard

Getting the right things done in the right amount of time is called being productive. How can you be more productive so that you can accomplish your goals? Make a list.

"Wow Alyson, you really stretched for that one when you wrote this book."

Okay, do not be a hater.

I know people have been making to-do lists for centuries. They have been doing it for so long because it works! When I was a marketing director, the best thing I ever did to improve my productivity, organization, and motivation was making a list. I do not mean a brief list on a Post-it Note. I mean developing what I now call my BGBoard.

My first BGBoard was a 4 x 8 sheet of acrylic plexiglass I bought from a local hardware store. I screwed it straight into the wall at work. After realizing that simply writing down everything I needed to do on the board was actually not helping me—instead, it was overwhelming and exhausting me—I came up with a formula that worked. Thus was born the BGBoard.

Here is how it works:

At the very top of the BGBoard, list your "BG"—big goal. If your BGBoard is at work, maybe you need to put your professional goal up top, but it may also be that you need to put your personal goal up top instead of, or in addition to, your professional goal. If you do not love your job but you need to keep it in order to feed your family right now, then put "healthy family" as your big goal, because at the end of the day, that is going to keep you motivated to go all in at work.

"But Alyson, what if someone walks by and sees my big goal?" So what. If they ask about it, tell them what you are doing. There is no shame in creating the life you want regardless of what anyone else might think or say. Now, with that being said, you have to use your brain. Do not write something on the board that would get you fired or in trouble.

Ultimately, the reason you put your big goal up top is that everything else you write down below it should put you closer to achieving that goal. Keeping that goal in front of your face every day will keep you motivated to go hard when the days get long and you just have to grind it out.

After you have set your big goals, use the space in the left middle area for The Grind. The Grind is where I kept up with my everyday tasks. There are two columns: The Daily Grind and The Weekly Grind. These lists change very often, so having the marker board makes it easy to update as needed. Under The Daily Grind, I write everything I have to do on a particular day. Under The Weekly Grind, I write everything that needs to be completed that week. As things get checked off the daily list, you move things over from the weekly list. The Grind is a constantly moving list. As you go through The Grind, keep your eye on the big goal so that you do not lose your motivation in the minutiae.

Do not lose your motivation in the minutiae.

The final key to staying organized and prioritizing is the 30-, 60-, 90-Day List on the right. You will keep a running list of what is coming up that you will need to work on. When you put this list on a board, you can see it all in one place—no scrolling, no flipping. As new options come up, you can see what the next three month's schedule looks like and decide if you need to add it to the list, say no, or just wait. Ultimately, whatever you put on your 30-, 60-, 90-Day List should feed The Grind, which should feed your big goal.

My board at work looked like this:

BIG GOALS

Increase Gen Z Customer Base

THE GRIND

Daily	Weekly	30 Days	60 Days	90 Days
Create .eps Logo	Order Camera	Create Social Content	Redesign Website	Add New Products

Once I had written everything out and prioritized it all on my BGBoard, I would put the Daily and 7-Day Grind tasks in my Google Calendar. That way I had it with me if I needed it even if I was away from my office.

The BGBoard worked so well that Joe and I put one up in our bedroom to keep us both organized and motivated to do what it takes every day to achieve our goals. And with it in our bedroom, as soon as we wake up we are able to see and focus on our *why*, because our big goal is written at the top of the board. Our *why* is what keeps us motivated. Our *why* is the reason we push. Our *why* is our big goal, and we are centering our life around making it happen. Another added bonus of having one in our bedroom is that we already know what our first moves need to be for the day to get us one step closer to crushing our big goal. We are not wasting time thinking and trying to figure out what we need to do—it is all already there!

BGBoards make prioritizing easy. You can erase and rewrite your list to get it in the order it needs to be as things come up...sick kids, emergency meetings, etc. And your big goals are always obvious, so you can make sure the things closest to the top of your list match what's at the top of your board—your goals.

When it comes to prioritizing the right way, I really like Stephen Covey's principle of *first things first*. Ultimately, whatever is at the top of your list should be feeding your goals, and that's where you should spend your time...nowhere else. Do not rob yourself of the time you need to accomplish your goals. Choose not to get caught up in side conversations, the deathly social media scroll, Netflix binges, online shopping, or anything else. You have to become hyperaware that what you're doing is actually getting you where and what you *really* want. If it doesn't, do not do it. Do not get distracted. That's a choice, so as you're going throughout your day own the ability to make decisions for you, not against you.

Your BGBoard only works if you take action to accomplish things on your board. As you mark steps off, your momentum will skyrocket and you will empower yourself with more focus and energy to level up your performance and kill it better and faster.

Going all in with your BGBoard allows you to dream bigger. As you begin crushing the goal(s) at the top of your board, then it is time to start thinking of what bigger and better objectives you could strive for.

When I was growing up, my big goal was to become an adult with a happy family who loved each other and enjoyed life together. I am so incredibly thankful I have achieved that goal. But a really exciting thing happens when you reach your goal(s)—your mind and your heart can start dreaming about even bigger possibilities. Now I am enjoying my family as I am dreaming and setting goals of how to make a bigger impact in this work. I am dreaming of helping people like you reach your goals, and here I am living it out. I want you to achieve your goals. I want you to dream bigger. I want you to take action right now. Go get a BGBoard and start taking your life to the next level. Your BGBoard does not have to be anything fancy. I told you mine was a piece of acrylic from a hardware store. Yours can be a piece of paper or a fancy mural on your wall if you are extra like that. Whatever it is, just take action and make it happen. When you get your BGBoard, I want to see it! I want to see your progress as you move things up and off your list as you crush your goals. Keep me updated on social @alysonvanhooser!

#QuittingTime

One of my biggest faults is I am a workaholic. That is not a humblebrag. I do not care how good something is—if you indulge in it too much, then you are stealing from more important things or parts of your life. When I say I am a workaholic, I mean that I can get so focused on work that I block out everything going on around me and keep my head down for hours. Where this becomes an issue for me is when I remember that my goals to be a good wife, mom, and friend are much more of a priority to me than to be successful professionally. More times than I want to think about, I have worked when I should have been playing with toddlers, chatting with friends, and dating my husband.

You too are probably going to have more than one goal, which means you will probably have to work on more than one goal in the same day. Your BGBoard will help you manage your organization and motivation. And setting a quitting time will help you keep your sanity through it all.

In full disclosure, I did not start doing this until after I had my third kid. It was like when my third kid was born, I realized that my oldest child was no longer a toddler girl; she had become my big girl. She was interacting with me in conversations as if she were a teenager. She was getting ready and showering all by herself. It all happened so fast I felt like I had worked her baby years away without even realizing it. So, now I set a quitting time. I fully quit one thing so I can focus on the next.

When work is over for the day, work is over. I do not try to do both when my kids get home after school. For three or four hours a night, I quit on work and I focus on being a mom. I put my phone away, and I do not answer calls or texts, because when I look at my goals, my family is at the top. Everything else can wait. But if you are like I was and you are trying to keep up with everything all the time, somewhere along the way someone or something is going to get the short end of the stick. I did not want that to be my family, so I set a quitting time.

You cannot do it all *all the time*. Your work needs you. Your people need you. You need you. Scheduling your quitting time will give you the freedom you need in your own mind to move from one thing to another. It will help you be completely present in the moment—more focused and therefore more efficient—so that you can make the most of the time you have. Your productivity as well as your quality of life will increase when you start setting a quitting time.

Today, take action to plan your quitting time. When are you going to fully check out of one thing so you can fully check into another?

#RadicallyExecute

Time is the variable that you can never change. You can never make more, and you are never guaranteed more. You cannot go back in time, and you cannot move forward in time. You have right now. You have the ability right now to choose to take action to start managing your time well. Managing your time well boils down to a series of choices throughout your day. You can choose to spend your time taking steps that will give you the results you really want, or you can choose to waste your time with distractions and actions that do not serve as progress toward your goals. Intentional action creates the possibility of dreams made reality. So friend, decide today to take action to manage your time well—get your BGBoard and set a quitting time—then radically execute on both. It is your choice. Own it!

Tool in this chapter: BGBoard

CHAPTER 15

EMPOWER OTHERS

There is not a 100 percent self-made person out there. You cannot reach all your goals on your own. It takes a village to make a success story. How do you start building your village? You give.

#HomeForTheSummer

When I was in elementary school, my dad went into rehab one summer. I do not remember where my brother went, but my sister and I went to live with "Mike and Rachel." I didn't know Mike and Rachel before we went to live with them. The only connection with them that I am aware of is that they had met my dad at church a few times.

I remember random details about those few months with Mike and Rachel. It was a happy home. I remember the Shania Twain music Rachel would play in the morning in her daughter's bedroom where me and my sister slept. I remember how they would get up and get ready for the day every morning—they weren't lying around doing nothing all the time; they were working. I remember sitting in the basement and staring at their carpet thinking how clean their house was. They took care of what they had. I remember watching how Mike and Rachel interacted: they were kind and patient with each other. I remember loving it there. It was peaceful. It felt safe. I could be a kid because everything else was taken care of. I remember thinking, *This will not last forever.* I remember thinking, *I better watch and learn so I know what to do when I grow up.*

And now, here I am with my own family, living the life I was dreaming of as a little girl. Now that I have three kids of my own, I have so much respect and appreciation for that young couple with young kids who went out of their way to help me when they knew a little girl couldn't give them anything in return.

I believe education empowers people to radically change their lives. Learning, whether it is through books or experiences, opens your mind to deeper understanding, unimagined possibilities, and the ability to believe you can do whatever you set your mind to.

Could I have found a way to make a better life for myself if I had never seen it? I cannot say for sure. But what I do know is that Mike and Rachel, along with many other people, have educated me indirectly. Through the experiences they gave me, I learned what I wanted and I learned how to get it. Because of that education by way of experience, my life differs dramatically from how statistics say it should be now. Because they and so many other people have given to me in one way or another, I would do anything for them at the drop of a hat. When you give, you build your army of people who will be willing to help you succeed.

Why a young couple with two babies of their own would take in two children they barely knew for a couple months I will never be able to explain. It was selfless, it was kind, and it was an experience that changed my perspective, which ultimately changed my life.

No matter how educated, talented, rich, or cool you are, how you treat people ultimately defines you. There is nothing more beautiful than someone who goes out of their way to make life beautiful for others.

It does not take a life-altering sacrifice on your part to make massive positive change in someone else's life. You can give a little or give a lot. Even the smallest effort can impact a life.

#EasyGiving

There are so many things you can do to empower the people around you that require little or no sacrifice on your part. I call that *easy giving*. There is absolutely no good reason why everyone should not be easy giving constantly.

Words. Words are free to give, too precious to take for granted, and too expensive to ever get back. The Bible says there is life and death in your words. The easiest way for you to ignite and fuel positive change in someone else's life is to use your words. It doesn't have to take a lot of resources (thought, time, money, etc.) to use your words to breathe life into people in these ways:

> Communicate the truth, kindly.

> Compliment others every chance you get.

> Always say "please" and "thank you."

> Provide encouragement.

> Willingly give positive direction.

Influence. Another way you can easily empower the people around you is to use your influence to open doors for them. Giving in this way just takes your making the effort to *think* of other people as opportunities come up for you to give. It will probably have very little effect on your own personal resources.

However, any time you have the authority to give a blessing through someone else's resources (a company, charity, etc.), you have to handle this very carefully—with integrity at all times.

You could use your influence to award someone a scholarship that you are the decision-maker on. You could promote someone who's earned it. You could choose to recommend a person to be selected for an opportunity to pursue higher education on the company's dime.

An old boss of mine nominated me to participate in the Leadership Kentucky program. I was not even aware of the program before he told me about it. The fact of the matter is that I would likely never have gotten in without his recommendation. His recommendation took only a few minutes of his time to make, but the experiences I had from the program opened my mind and heart to great new things. I am forever grateful.

#HurtsSoGood

You can give to the people around you at a level where you feel the pain from what you're giving up but the joy you get from it overshadows any pain you might feel.

A great example of that is money.

You can pay for the car behind you when you are at a drive-thru. You can give money to a church or charitable organization. You can sponsor a clean water well in a Third World country. You can pay for a child to play sports or get new clothes.

I have been incredibly blessed over the years by the people who have given their financial resources to me. Churches have kept the water running in my house as a child. People have paid for me to play little league sports, get yearbooks at school, and fill my backpack with school supplies. I could go on and on about the generosity I have experienced in my life. I did not deserve any of it, but I am so thankful for selfless people who gave me the opportunity to have the things I needed as well as some of the things that just make life more enjoyable as a kid.

When you give money to help people meet their needs, you create positive experiences for them. Those positive experiences equip and empower them to strive for more.

#DeepSacrifice

Time is a resource you can never get back…never.

I'll never forget picture day in third grade. My teacher kept me after school the day before and rolled my hair in foam rollers. I felt like a princess. I know the happiness and excitement had to be oozing from every ounce of my eight-year-old body. She saw a little girl who could use some love from a mother figure and she decided to give her time to me…something she could never get back. I am sold out for Mrs. Conger simply for that one thing. But I have to tell you that the next morning, when I took the rollers out before school to see my curls, I thought putting lots of mousse on my hair would help the curls stay put. Remember, I got myself ready in the mornings. No one was there to tell me that putting wet mousse on dry hair would completely take out the curls and leave my hair crunchy. It wasn't the hair day I expected for picture day that year, but the experience the night before was priceless and I'll never forget it.

As my kids become school age, I am looking forward to the opportunity to be able to pour into their friends' lives just like so many did for me when I was young. You see, when you give, you are helping the person you're giving, you are filling your own soul, you are creating your army, but you are also impacting more people than you could ever even know.

Deep sacrifices can also be giving up something you really want or ignoring your personal needs so that someone else can get what they want. This is most often done in parenting. I know I would do whatever it takes to help my children reach their full potential. But there have been people who have deeply sacrificed for me to whom I have no relation. I do not know why these people have crossed my path—you may call it fate; I say it is part of God's plan—but the reason I am here pouring into you today is because so many people poured into me.

When my dad abandoned me at 13 and left me with his friends, they immediately showed me love. They deeply sacrificed their time, their money, and their emotional bandwidth so that I could thrive... so that I didn't have to go into foster care. When everything hit the fan and the government made me move in with a blood relative, they fought for me. I watched. I heard. I will never forget. They can never get back what they gave up when they chose to love on me, but I am forever changed. I will continue to honor them. I am sold out, all in, part of their army for life.

When you deeply sacrifice for someone else, that is love. Love makes life worth living for people on both the giving and the receiving end.

#HowMuchToGive

Most people I know are very willing to give to other people. I bet you are too. The question is, how much should you give?

There may be times you have had or will have opportunities to give to other people, but you are hesitant because you do not know if they will use your gift in what *you* think is the right way. That's not your burden to bear. You do not know if the kid you're helping will end up taking the right path—give anyway. You do not know what that person asking for money will really do with it—give anyway. You do not know if you are smart enough to help—try anyway. If you're presented with an opportunity to give, and you can, then you should. I believe somehow, some way, that there are positive dividends traced back to you or for you when you give.

But then there are times when you should say no.

You have to be fully aware of your resources—emotional, mental, financial, physical, and temporal. Your resources are not unlimited. No matter what level of giving you *want* to do, if your tank is empty, you will not have anything to give when you really want or need to. *(Head back to Chapter 11 for more on taking care of yourself.)*

Go back to the law you laid down for yourself in Chapter 2. When you are deciding how much you can give to work, to your community, to your church, to your troubled friend or family member, you have to answer this question for yourself: Am I willing to sacrifice my goals to make sure someone else can have what they want/need?

Now, there will be small things like buying a police officer's lunch that will not take much time or consideration or sacrifice to make it happen. But if you are presented with a deep sacrifice, that will take some time to think about.

The trajectory of my life has been pointed in the right direction because people decided it was worth it to them to make a deep sacrifice for someone else at that time. I, in turn, have chosen to live my life in a way that will honor that going forward. Giving to others is not always about filling your own cup, but filling someone else's. You never know what your sacrifice will mean in the life of someone else...and the lives they will touch going forward.

However, there will likely come a point when someone else asks something of you and that little voice inside you speaks up and says, "No." More often than not, we do not say "no"; we say "yes" and are dying inside because of it. We end up stressed to the max, overwhelmed, anxious, angry...the list goes on.

You do not have to live that way. You can say "no" in a kind way. You can thank them for thinking of you and tell them you are really trying to keep your priorities in line and you have a full plate right now. You might also have to say "no" firmly. Some people will push you—do not give in. You have to protect yourself and those closest to you. You have to take care of your resources so you can survive and support the people around you.

You should give. I should give. But do not just deplete your resources blindly. Keep the law you laid down for yourself in mind. Do not be afraid to say "no," and jump on every chance you can to say "yes."

#MassiveImpact

When you give, you ignite power within other people. That power can help them reach their own goals, and it can help you reach yours. It's a win-win.

It doesn't take grand gestures to radically change someone's life. Your small moves can make a massive impact.

When your life is over, what will it all have meant if you never do anything beyond yourself? So take care of yourself, but find ways to jump on every chance you can to give to other people.

I believe kindness is key to a satisfied soul. Kindness is not a feeling; it is an action. Actions are made by choice. Will you own your ability to make a difference in the lives around you?

CHAPTER 16

BE BOLD

When I was 13, I wanted a tattoo. I saw someone else with one and thought I would instantly fit in with the cool crowd at school if I got a tattoo. The fear of my dad telling me "no" was nowhere near as powerful as my desire to get that tattoo, so I planned out how I was going to ask my dad the big question the whole bus ride home from school. This conversation was going to set the tone for how I handled myself in business and in my relationships from this point forward.

After a 30-minute bus ride, the best *ask* I, a 13-year-old child, could come up with was, "Dad, can I get a tattoo? I already know what I want." Not knowing how he was going to respond, I waited.

He looked up at me from the couch after thinking about it for a second, and he said, "Yes."

I was shocked! A few days later, I walked down the street with my dad and got my first tattoo at "Booboo's Tattoos."

From that moment on, I became an unabashed evangelist for boldly asking specifically for what you want. You know what—I am actually passionate about bold moves in general. Just because you do not know what the outcome may be does not mean you should not jump. You may just get exactly what you have been dreaming of—or better!

Why are so many people unwilling to make bold moves? Most often, I hear explanations that stem back to insecurity. You may say, "I am too shy," or "They will turn me down," or "I am just not confident enough." I call bull. All of that is just an excuse. Being bold is not a gift or a trait; it is a choice. You decide to either own it or not. You have to act your way into feelings, not feel your way into action. The only way to become bold is to start taking bold action, making bold choices.

> **Being bold is not a gift or a trait; it is a choice.**

#BoldMoves

Do not let your nerves limit you and keep you from making bold moves. You have to decide to take action to level up.

If you think something bad or, alternatively, something monumental is about to happen, your internal physical body will react. You have probably heard the term "fight or flight." When you think or feel like something big or bad is about to happen, your body will instinctively go into fight-or-flight mode. Your sympathetic nervous system will scream to your adrenal glands: I NEED ADRENALINE! As the adrenaline shoots through your body, your heart rate, blood pressure, and breathing rate all skyrocket in order to prime you for what is about to happen. And even when the threat is finally gone, it will take you about 20–60 minutes to chill out.

The next time you need to speak up for yourself or make a bold move, I have two actions you can take to counteract the fight-or-flight mode. These actions will help you calm down so that you can show up like a boss. If at all possible, I want you to start doing these at least 20 minutes before you go in for the ask or to make the move:

1. Move!

When I first started speaking to company executives, I would get so nervous. My heart would be pounding so hard I just knew I was about to internally combust. I would be entirely in my head, trying to go over my presentation, but there was a constant background voice saying, *What if I forget? What if my voice is going to be too shaky? What if they ask me questions I do not know the answer to? What if I am not prepared for this?* It was chaos in my brain! My father-in-law, who is a Hall of Fame keynote speaker, told me that I need to let out a little energy beforehand. So what did I start doing? I would go up and down the stairs a few times as fast as I could before a presentation. I have done jumping jacks in the private bathroom. I even shut my office door and did push-ups one time. Honestly, it helped. I could not think about anything else for just a moment, except for the exercise I was doing. The exercise helped the nerves wear off enough for me to be able to think clearly. So the next time you're about to go into a big meeting or make a huge presentation, get your body moving right before it and you'll feel the difference so you can go in calm, cool, and collected.

2. Breathe!

When you start panicking mentally, your body will react. Your nervous system will start firing and your heart rate will go up, your blood pressure will go up, and you will start breathing faster. It's incredible how your mind can control your body. This physical reaction to visual or mental stress can be great when you are in danger, but if you're not, it leaves you feeling panicked and restricted. How do you combat that? You breathe. There is not a one-time action you can take to reduce your heart rate or your blood pressure, but you can control your breathing. Breathe in deeply, hold it for a moment, and exhale slowly. Do this over and over. Concentrate on breathing, nothing else. Even if you have to say, "In, in, in, in, in, hold it, hold it, hold it, out, out, out, out, out" in order to give yourself something to concentrate on, do it. When you slow your breathing down you are sending a message to your nervous system that everything is okay, so it will calm down.

#OwnYourOpportunity

You create your own opportunity by putting in the work to seek it out, prepare for it, and get noticed for it. Yes, you have to be bold, and you have to ask for doors to be opened and chances to be given. But before you make your bold move and ask for an opportunity, you have to first prepare and execute way beyond expectation. Here are a few things you need to do *before* you make a bold ask or move.

1. Put in the work.

I do not mean just show up and do your job; I mean you must do more than is expected of you. This can apply at work and at home.

When I was seven months pregnant with my third child, my blood pressure was out of control. I was in and out of the hospital multiple times during the last two months of my pregnancy. Each time I would go in, they would keep me for observation. Once my blood pressure lowered, they would send me home. It did not matter if I got home at 7:00 P.M. or 4:00 A.M., I showed up to work the next day. Did my boss expect me there? Absolutely not, but I chose to put in the work and come in anyway. Did I necessarily want to? No. Did I feel like it? Pregnant and sleep-deprived, I most certainly did not. But I chose to take action that would get me closer to my goals instead of farther away.

I finally had to have an emergency C-section six weeks before my due date. My baby boy ended up staying in the NICU for a while and he needed longer one-on-one care when I finally brought him home. When I met with my boss to ask him about taking off longer with the baby, do you think he let me have the extra time while holding my job? Yes, he did. He did because I put in the work beforehand and saved my ask for when I needed it most.

How can you put in the work today to prepare a reputation that warrants success and opportunities in the future?

2. Ask questions.

Asking questions can be a strategic move—and when done in the right way, can make you look smart rather than clueless. If done correctly, you can get the information and answers you want and potentially increase your own credibility with the people around you. Wise people ask calculated questions. How can you formulate effective questions to drive your success? Below are two guidelines.

Number 1 — Be sure to ask questions only if you have been paying attention. I have been in multiple meetings where we were knee-deep into a conversation and then suddenly someone speaks up and asks a question that was just answered. It then becomes obvious to everyone in the room that the person was not paying attention. That is not the position you want to be in.

Number 2 — Make sure your question moves the conversation forward. Don't ask a question just to hear yourself talk. For example, a good question would be asking for more details about something in order to get you and/or others closer to clarity on the subject under discussion. A bad example of asking for more details about something would be if the question and answer bears no weight in the matter at hand.

I'll give you a quick example. If you are in a meeting and you are discussing a customer service situation with an employee, do not be the person who brings up the question of, "Did you hear that customer John Doe got in trouble with the police this weekend?" That question has nothing to do with the customer service issue at hand. It's irrelevant. It's wasting time. It's hurting your reputation if you cannot discern what is appropriate and relevant and what is not.

Those who ask calculated questions are more likely to move closer to crushing their goals. So the next time you get ready to ask a question, calculate! Do the math: $1 + 2 =$ win.

3. Seek out educational opportunities.

I told you that I was previously in a marketing position I did not want initially. In order to still learn and grow in the direction I wanted my career to go, I had to seek out opportunities to learn outside of what my marketing responsibilities required. I went to my boss and asked him if I could attend a meeting in the organization that involved a committee I was not on. The committee was made up of VPs and board members. It is not like I belonged there, but I wanted to be there so I could learn. I made that clear to my boss. Did he give me permission to come, sit, listen, and learn? Yes.

When you focus on learning more, you can be more.

I never would have had that opportunity to learn and develop a deeper understanding of the organization and our industry had I not made a bold move and asked to go to the meeting. The knowledge I gained from the information and conversations in that room still sticks with me today. When you focus on learning more, you can be more.

4. See opportunities no one else can.

I had been in my management role a little over a year when the CEO asked all the managers to complete a succession plan. If you aren't familiar with what a succession plan is, basically it answers the question of who will take your place when you get promoted, quit, or get hit by a train—however you want to look at it.

As I started digging into the analytics of my department, I discovered that customer traffic was down. Managers across our team had the bandwidth to manage more employees. There were also multiple projects we should be working on that would add to our bottom line. What did all of this mean? It meant that the research showed there was no need for my current position. I was a new employee, a young employee. This was my first big project at this company, and all the research I had done came down to *this!* I did not want to present my succession plan and say, "You should fire me." I had to have a job!

So I figured out a way to make this a win-win for everyone. I started lining out the organization's weaknesses and paired them with my strengths. There were problems I could fix. There were value strategies and projects I could implement and manage that would add to the bottom line! There was my opportunity.

When the time came, I stood in front of senior management in the boardroom and gave them what they asked for—a personal recommendation for who could effectively fill my current position and why. They were all pleased. But then I turned my presentation from tradition to innovation. Some of their faces went from smiles of support...to shock. I thoroughly explained to them how the numbers of the business proved there was no longer a need for my current position within the company. The only reason to keep me in that current role would be because "That's the way we've always done it." And that way was not helping the business.

I went on to explore important unmet needs within the company and shared my idea for how a new position could address them. They saw the needs and agreed. Then I stepped up to the plate and asked for opportunity. I was sweating bullets and my heart was racing, but I gave them every reason as to why I was the best fit for this new position. I closed the presentation by asking for the opportunity to fill this new position. The room was silent. I left that meeting without direction or feedback. It was brutal.

However, executive management finished out the fiscal year by eliminating my current position and creating a new, more strategic, more profitable position within the company.

Who got the new job? I did.

When you can see opportunities that no one else can, people will open doors to let you soar.

#ItDidntWork

Owning your potential is about seeking out opportunities and education and then putting in the work. If you do not do those three things and you show up and make a bold move or ask, it might not work out like you had hoped.

I had a friend come in my office day after day, month after month, unhappy about how much money she was making. She didn't want to leave, but she was starting to look for another job because she wasn't making enough money to support the lifestyle she wanted.

She would always ask me how I got to where I am. I told her it was because I asked for the opportunities I wanted. Finally, she decided to take action and go ask for a raise.

What happened? Her supervisor talked to me a few days later and mentioned what went down. She told me she asked for the raise, but she wasn't going to get it. Here was her logic: she was already getting a cost of living increase every year. Her job responsibilities had not changed since she was hired. She had not sought out more ways to benefit the company her entire time there. So, her asking for a raise for doing the exact same work was not going to net her the result she wanted.

When I advised her to go ask for what she wanted, I assumed she was finding newer and better ways to do things, making positive suggestions, and changing things up for the better. I figured she was going above and beyond and simply not getting her value. I was wrong.

I had to finish this conversation with her. She had no idea I had talked to her supervisor about it all. (*Her supervisor and I were on the same level, so we could discuss certain things that you absolutely cannot discuss with people who are below you in the organizational chart. I do leadership training about this, so if that conversation piques your interest, reach out to me about going deeper.*) I asked her, "Has your job changed? Have you offered up anything new or more valuable to the department?" Her answer was "No." She came in and did the job she was hired for. She thought that she deserved a raise. She was wrong.

Doing the basics, just meeting the standard expectations, will not catapult you toward your goals personally or professionally. It is when you do something beyond what anyone expects that they will take notice and jump at the opportunity to give you a shot. That is how you own it.

#WhyNot

YOU control your success. You can choose to wait for opportunity, or you can create it. You can choose to be fearless and go after what you want. You can choose to shine your light brightly no matter who is trying to put it out. My question to you is, why not be bold enough to make it happen?

CHAPTER 17

BYE FELICIA

If you have _BEEF_ with somebody, you all are not enjoying hamburgers together—you've got issues with each other.

Whether it is your issue or theirs, how you handle drama affects you, the people around you, and your potential future opportunities. Drama gets in the way of moving forward to crush your goals. Unless your goal is to be on reality TV, you need to kill the beef.

> "Drama does not just walk into your life.
> Either you create it, invite it,
> or associate with it."
> —Unknown

You have the power to control the amount of drama in your life. You just have to own the responsibility of getting rid of it. Less drama means a straighter path to achieving your goals.

I once heard someone say that the only way to deal with a toxic person is "do not play." I get the essence of that statement...you do not want to play into and elevate the drama. But you absolutely cannot ignore it. You have to take action. You have to take intentional, mature, results-driven action to take control of the situation so it doesn't control you and your future.

Here are three tips to help you get rid of drama.

#GetOverYourself

I know it sounds harsh to hear *get over yourself*, but I am hoping that by shooting you straight, you will be able to clearly see and know what you need to do before it is too late.

If you are the one with the issue, you have got to decide if the battle you're fighting is pushing for or against your goals. If the issue is irrelevant to what you really want to accomplish, let it go. Do not be your own worst enemy.

On the other hand, I understand that you may be caught up in the middle of drama that is not your fault, but if you do not want it to negatively affect you, then you have to take responsibility for fixing it. The only reason you wouldn't fix it would boil down to your pride or ego, and feeding those two monsters will lead nowhere good. If that's what has kept you from doing what it takes to kill the beef, you have got to get over yourself, because that approach doesn't work in your favor in the long run.

What issues are you facing that you *could* fix if you just chose to own the responsibility for making it right? If you do not take control, what opportunities could you be missing out on?

Ultimately, when it comes to drama, you are either going to make a choice for yourself or against yourself. Do not forget the law you laid down in Chapter 2. Remember who you are and what you really want. Drama isn't on the plan to get you there.

#RootIssue

Now that you have got the first step—choosing to get over yourself and own the responsibility to make it right—the next step is to get to the heart of the issue.

The thing is, symptoms of issues can show up in different ways: a rude comment in a meeting, a lack of communication between departments, disengaged co-workers, family members who never call, the promotion you are never selected for, etc. But you cannot fix an issue if you know only what the symptoms are.

> **You cannot fix an issue if you know only what the symptoms are.**

You have to get down to the root of it all, or else you'll keep spinning your wheels, putting Band-Aids on what you think are shallow cuts but are actually much deeper.

I worked with a woman named "Beth." After we hired a new girl, Beth went from sweetheart to sourpuss fast. You could tell Beth was irritated from the moment she walked in the door—the look on her face, the way she sat her purse down, how she talked to co-workers. You know what I mean.

Beth had a lot going on at home, so we assumed she just couldn't leave it at the door. We all ate lunch together, so we would try to engage her and help by asking about what was going on at home and offering suggestions. Nothing would give with her. It got to the point where her attitude was affecting the whole department, even customers.

Finally, in a meeting, everything hit the fan and Beth lost her professionalism...but we got down to the root issue. Beth's home life wasn't the issue. Instead, because of the new girl we hired, Beth felt she was being pushed into the background and becoming a less valuable part of our team.

Our efforts to help fix her home life were not doing anything to kill the beef at work. But once we knew what the root issue was, we could start making the right moves to make things better.

If you want to control drama and conflict, do not ignore it and let it continue to fester. Get down to the root issue so you can fix it.

Through my years of experience working in multiple management roles, in multiple industries, with multiple generations, I learned that the best way to get to the heart of an interpersonal issue is to approach it privately, with humility and kindness.

When there becomes an issue between you and someone else, ask to have a private conversation with them. You should always handle negative situations in private.

Once you're alone, tell them you genuinely want to understand why you guys are not jiving so that you can make things right. This immediately shows them that you are not looking to fuel the fire but to snuff it out. It also—whether it's your fault or not—makes them feel you like you are not placing blame but searching for a solution.

Remember to use kind words, a kind tone of voice, and have a kind demeanor. You cannot make people do certain things, but you can control the factors that come into their decision-making process by the way you handle yourself. When you do this, it will help create an environment where the other person feels comfortable enough to let their guard down and open up. Once that happens, you both can get down to the real issue at hand so you can move on—and move up!

#BeTheSolution

When you are having that private conversation with someone, taking the responsibility to make it right—even if it is not your fault—is key to smoothing things over going forward.

You have to ask them how you can fix the problem. Asking them for the solution does a couple things. Namely, it shows them that you're coming in with a humble attitude, which will help them be more on offense rather than on defense, where progress is stalled.

When they give you an answer, do not buck. This may mean you have to lose the messy bun, or stop cursing at work, or that you have to add more fluff into your conversation rather than always just getting down to business. Be open to their concerns. The goal is to eradicate the issue, so unless it compromises your integrity, ethics, morals, professionalism, or the goals you have, do it—own it!

Drama will suck the life out of you mentally, emotionally, physically, and professionally about as quick as anything. The way I figured out how to effectively deal with the situations I kept ending up in as a child was to just turn my brain off. It was almost like I could flip a switch, tell myself to toughen up, do not look, do not feel, do not think…and eventually whatever was going on would be over and I could come back to life.

That approach—basically, ignoring whatever is going on—will not stop the drama in and around you. It may help you deal in the moment, but just "dealing" will not push you forward to reach your goals; it will leave you stuck. You have to own this and choose to be the solution to squashing drama—for the good of your team, organization, family, etc., yes; but also for YOU.

Do not let someone else's negative attitude and actions rob you of getting what you want. It's absolutely and 100 percent a choice that you control. Will you own it?

CHAPTER 18

NOT THIRSTY, JUST THRIVING

Connecting with your people is the fuel that drives leadership success.

> Thirsty: adj. Desire, greed, obsession, or lust for an object or person characterized by overeagerness or obsessiveness (negative connotation)

Your journey to success is more like a conversation than a monologue. Hear me carefully: you have to take responsibility for appropriately controlling the conversation and keeping it moving forward, but the other people involved in the conversation can enrich the dialogue. They can make it easier, more fun, more fulfilling. But they can only do that if you give them the chance to be involved.

Let's dig into exactly why you should constantly be looking to build more relationships in order to be successful. Doing this doesn't make you seem thirsty. Instead, it will make you thrive. Networking is a win-win.

> **Networking:** verb. The action or process of interacting with others to exchange information and develop professional or social contacts

#MemoryLane

I didn't even know until well into my career that there was a fancy business word for making friends, but there is: *networking.*

The connections I have made throughout my life continue to provide opportunities and blessings for me. Let me take you on a bird's-eye view of my professional journey:

I met Joe in a P.E. class as a sophomore in high school. Because of his mad dodgeball skills in class, he and I started dating then and have been together ever since. I didn't know what I wanted to major in when I went to college, but his parents suggested a business degree. So, I got a Business Management & Marketing degree. That degree opened the door for me to get a job as a management trainee right out of college.

I went to church with "John Williams." John contacted me out of the blue about nine months after college graduation and offered me a management position for an international retailer. I took it! That job allowed me and Joe to be able to buy our first house. While going through the loan process, I met Matt. Matt, you'll recall, offered me a management position at the bank that later turned into a marketing director position. It was a better opportunity for my family, so I took that job. When I quit the retail management job under John, John's wife started watching my kids. She now loves them like her own and is like a second mother to them. My kids would have never known her if I hadn't connected with them at church years before.

Matt nominated me for Leadership Kentucky, and I was chosen for the program. The LKY experience allowed me to build friendships with people in politics and keyed me in to the possibility of my getting involved in government one day. The program also opened my eyes to the impact of government on the success or failure of communities. Because of the connection with Matt and the opportunities I had while I worked for him, specifically LKY, I developed a deep passion for serving my community and I was elected to serve on the city council at 27 years old.

Because I was having such a positive experience and impact through my position on the city council, I was approached by Jack to be a commercial insurance agent for his company. I left the bank and took the new opportunity.

My tough experiences, coupled with my professional and political experience, gave me opportunities to spread my message on motivation, success, leadership and professionalism. I became more and more interested in what Joe's dad does for a living as a professional speaker and author. In 2018, I went to work with him doing what I now love.

I was BFFs with "Jane Smith" in elementary school. I became really close with the entire Smith family from a young age. Twenty-plus years later, the mother of the Smith family gave me my very first professional speaking opportunity. That first speaking engagement gave me the kickstart I needed for a successful speaking career.

None of that would have happened if I didn't have my act together. And I couldn't have my act together if I wouldn't have chosen to level up and own it since I was a little girl. Also, it is evident by all the twists and turns on my journey that I wouldn't be where I am today had I not built relationships with people along the way. And no, I didn't know that the friendships I was making in elementary school would help my career later in life. But I am older and smarter now, and I realize the power of connections. The more people you know, the more opportunities you can get and give. I will, for the rest of my life, push people to network constantly. As you can see, there is so much value in it!

> **The more people you know, the more opportunities you can get and give.**

#YourRelationshipWithYourself

I haven't always been a fan of building relationships on purpose.

Joe and I both laugh because the first thing he ever said to me, passing me in the hallway in high school, was, "You need to smile more." Needless to say, I was less than impressed.

The fact of the matter is, at the time when he saw me and I didn't look happy, it was because I wasn't. That was not long after my dad left and I was being passed from house to house. But deeper than that, I felt like I needed to harden up so I could push through. I had no desire to make new friends or build relationships. Who would have wanted a relationship with me anyway? My life was and always had been a hot mess. No one deserved to be brought into that.

With A LOT of persistence, Joe broke through that wall. But it wasn't until I became a mom that I really realized that there was even a wall there. You know how I realized it? I started wanting to hug people. I NEVER wanted to hug people before that. You'd never know it now, but I wasn't a touchy-feely person growing up. We do not have to dig into the psychology of that right now. But becoming a mother unlocked a part of me I didn't know existed. So when I have an opportunity to meet someone new, I take it. You never know what they are going through and how you might be able to help.

The benefit of networking is that while you should never give of yourself solely to get something in return, sometimes when you do, others are willing to give in return—and that's pretty cool.

The ability to go out and build relationships starts with the relationship you have with yourself. That will set the tone for every other relationship you have, will have, or will not have. Let down your walls, care about other people, help and be helped. All of that is a choice. Own it.

#HowDoYouNetwork

1. Get to know _____.

There are people you come in contact with every day. The person in the office you do not know well, the waitress at lunch, the person on the elevator. Focus on getting to know the people you naturally come in contact with every day.

Then there are the people you are going to have to make an effort to reach out to in order to start a connection.

I remember the first time I purposefully reached out and straight up said, "I am trying to network." Okay, I didn't say it exactly like that.

When I first started thinking about getting involved in government, I wanted to get insider tips from someone who was doing it well. Tom was a judge executive in a neighboring county, and from everything I could tell through the media, he was killing it. He and I were friends on Facebook. He was very active on the platform, so I knew he would get my message if I sent one there. I typed out a long message asking if he would like to go to lunch one day. I told him I had been keeping up with him in regards to his judge exec role and I'd love the opportunity to get to know and learn from him.

He agreed to go to lunch, but I could tell from the moment he walked into the restaurant that he thought something was up. I mean, the man was in politics, so I know now from my own political experience that there are a lot of people out there with negative intentions masked with positivity. After a few minutes, I broke the tension and just said, "Tom, I have no agenda. You are a high performer, and I am hoping that by having a conversation with you that some of your good mojo will rub off. That's it." He humbly laughed. We ate all the tacos and chips and salsa. It was a great lunch. He and I still stay in touch today. I have learned so much from him over the past several years.

2. Make the first move.
It is not awkward; it's impressive.

Like Tom, I have found that most people, if you simply ask, are more than happy to help and to teach.

I feel like the word *awkward* describes how most people feel, or are afraid the other person will feel, about meeting new people, especially when you're the first person making the move.

Making the first move is not awkward; it's impressive. Your heart may be pounding, your mind may be going crazy with anxious thoughts, but you have got to crush those thoughts and feelings. Building a bigger network will help you reach your goals because it will open doors to opportunities you may never get otherwise…maybe ones you didn't even know you wanted!

> *Making the first move is not awkward; it's impressive.*

3. Build rapport.

We have to refer back to Chapter 5 on this one. You have to understand and adapt to the people around you in order to really be able to build rapport.

For me, like I said in Chapter 1, I am a person who studies people, and I have done that since I was just a child. I started mirroring people who were getting and living the way I wanted. When I did that, I started getting the results I wanted. As I got older, it became natural for me to adapt to the people I was around. Again, I was not changing who I was as far as the law I laid down for myself, but I would adapt my body language, the words I used, and the things I would talk about depending on whom I was talking to.

The concept of mirroring and matching people is nothing new. Now, you do not need to be like Andy on *The Office*—he took it too far. He went from mirroring to sucking up way too hard, really fast. However, you should be hyperaware of the subtleties going on around you all the time.

One thing I constantly talk about, even at home with my family, is their "second face." I was first introduced to the concept of a second face in my college psychology class, and it was fascinating to me. Let me give you an obvious example of the second face…

My son Lincoln likes to sneak bugs into the house or anywhere close to me so that he can laugh as I lose every ounce of my dignity running away from one. Lincoln can walk up to me with his hands in a fist. If I ask him, "Lincoln, do you have a bug in your hand?" and he says, "No" with a straight face…but I can see in his eyes that he is kidding—THAT is his second face, the face that, try as you might, you just cannot hide.

You have to pay attention to people's second face in order to build rapport.

People's second face will tell you when you have said something wrong. People's second face will tell you if they like you. People's second face will tell you if they are ready for you to stop talking or if they are all in with you. Recognizing people's second face goes back to becoming hyperaware. If you are looking for a deeper signal from a person, you will find it if you make yourself aware of their second face. When you can pick up on people's nuances, it will help you match and mirror them and, therefore, build rapport that turns into a stronger connection. That's good networking.

4. Follow up...thank-you cards, birthdays, meetings.

Before you leave that first interaction, find a way to stay connected. Whether it be planning a lunch meeting or connecting on social media, nail down a way to stay in touch. If it is more of a personal relationship you're building, connecting on Instagram, Twitter, Snapchat, and/or Facebook is appropriate. If it is more of a professional relationship, I would suggest connecting with them on LinkedIn.

After you have moved past the first couple of interactions, you can take the relationship to a more structured place. You can put things like their birthday or work anniversary on your calendar so that you remember to reach out to them to recognize these special occasions. This is a natural way for you to keep the connection strong.

Do not forget to take inventory of who the person is you are connecting with before you reach out. You will need to tailor your approach to their preferences. If you know they don't like talking on the phone, don't call them on their birthday...send them a text. Something that never goes out of style and looks great on your part—a handwritten card. Whether it is a thank-you note, birthday card, anniversary card, etc., it is always good to up your game by adding this personal touch, so get in the habit of sending cards. People will remember if you make the effort to stay connected, because most people do not.

5. If something comes up and they would be a good fit, give them a shot.

The best thing about networking is being able to share opportunities with other people. This blesses other people and feeds your own soul.

It is important that you are constantly building relationships with new people because as you move forward in your career and in your life, you undoubtedly will have the opportunity to open doors for someone else. If your network is small, you may not know anyone for whom you can open a door. You may be in a management position and need a really good employee, but if you haven't built a big network, you may not know anyone who would be a good fit. Then you're left with nothing.

Not only does networking enable you to give; it can also help you reach your own goals. However, do not wait to give until you get. Focus on giving, and then if you can get something back from it, that's an added benefit. There will be times where you give and give and give and never get anything in return. Give anyway. The emotional benefits you will receive from that attitude will positively affect your life, and that in itself makes giving worthwhile.

#NotAwkwardJustImpressive

Relationships with people are what make life worth living. Whether it is personally or professionally, the more people you know, the more opportunities you will have. The opportunity you are looking for may be personal fulfillment, such as love or friendship, or it may be more professionally focused, e.g., so you can get to the next level in your career. Either way, build new relationships with this win-win approach. Focus on giving more than you get and being thankful when the relationship does give back to you.

Successfully networking to reach your goals boils down to a choice to make intentional moves to meet new people and stay in touch. You have got to level up and own your ability to create opportunities for yourself. Purposefully building relationships will help you do that. Networking is not awkward. It helps you crush your goals, and that, my friend, is impressive.

CHAPTER 19

MAKE YOUR
OWN HYPE

When you decide to take full responsibility for your life, nobody can rob you of your power to achieve your dreams. You—and only you—get to choose what you will do and who you will become from this moment forward. I do not know about you, but I am not a betting person. There are so many unknown variables in life, but if there was ever one thing I was going to bet on…I would bet on me.

I want you to do the same thing. I want you to give this everything you've got in you and bet on yourself. You cannot lose. Owning it is the one thing you can control above all else. Ultimately, you are the most influential person in your life. You decide if you are going to step up to the plate and change the whole game or if you are going to stay on the sidelines while other people keep winning.

Everything you do from this moment forward will be a choice. A choice either for yourself or against yourself. A decision to get one step closer to your goals or one step further away. For you to own it, you have to be in a state of hyperawareness constantly. That is the only way you can make the right choices so you can gain the momentum needed to make your dreams a reality. This is all you.

> **You are the most influential person in your life.**

#Hype

I watched a video on Instagram of J.Lo after a workout. She said, "Cannot nobody motivate me! You have got to be your own hype!" She is so right. I mean, she was talking about squatting with weights, and I am talking about crushing your goals, but the point remains the same.

There is the possibility that you will wake up tomorrow, or next week, or next month, and you will not feel excited about what you need to do that day to crush your goals. You might be tempted to choose the easy way out. You might go halfway or simply give up on yourself.

You cannot forget who you are when you wake up in the morning! Do not be deceived by your feelings, because from the moment your eyes open, the clock is ticking and you either progress or regress. There is no middle ground. There is no treading water until you feel like moving in the right direction again. If you are treading water, you are in the snail-pace process of dying. You have to own it right now, own it on the hard days, own it on the days when you just do not want to anymore. Say to yourself, *This is how I feel, but this is how I am going to act.* You do not feel your way into positive action. Instead, you act on your goals regardless of your feelings.

You create your own hype when you start making decisions and taking action that gets you closer to reaching your goals. Things will start snowballing in the best way. Your momentum will grow as you roll forward. Small wins will lead to massive victories. The day will come when you are not fighting against things in your way but instead busting through them without even realizing the roadblocks were there.

Still afraid you might fall off your path, get distracted, maybe even give up on yourself? It's time to clean house—literally and figuratively.

#CleanHouse

You know when your friends text and say they are dropping by for a surprise visit and you run around the house like a maniac, cleaning things you haven't touched in months, vacuuming and dusting like there is someone chasing you, and 30 minutes later your house looks better than it has in weeks? You are about to do that with your life. There are physical things you are going to have to get rid of to make sure you are creating an environment for success, not failure.

I grew up in a mess. When I was a little kid, for several years we did not have a stove in our house. Where the stove was supposed to be in the kitchen was just an empty area on the wall. There was a washer and dryer in a closet in the kitchen, and I cannot tell you why, but all our clothes would end up piled higher than the countertop in the space where the oven should have been. I would wake up in the morning to get me and my younger sister ready for school, and I would have to dig in that pile on the kitchen floor to find what we were going to wear.

Our house was in such disarray that people would come over and clean it for us. I do not mean maids, either. I mean social workers would give an ultimatum and then church volunteers, nice people in the community, and even extended family would come help get things in decent order. When your environment is a mess, from the moment you open your eyes you are smacked in the face with chaos. Everything is out of order before you can even get started.

As I have grown up and started living on my own, I saw how a clean environment can change your entire approach to life. When your room, your house, your car, your office, your desk are in order, then you can spend time thinking and doing things that get you closer to your goals. You will not have to waste time constantly fighting to get back to zero so you can start doing things that will get you closer to your goals.

Everybody has a crazy schedule. Planning is your friend. You and that BGBoard need to be tight. I schedule everything—and I mean *everything*. So put it on your board and plan your day. Grind it out and get your stuff cleaned up. Keep it cleaned up. When you do this, you are choosing to give yourself a place where you can grow instead of die.

While you're *cleaning house*, you have to think about more than just your floors, walls, and tabletops. Take inventory of everything you consume, because what you put in will affect what you put out. You are either fueling or depleting your best resources by what you consume.

It is time to clean house when it comes to the music you listen to. Music is powerful. I believe every lyric matters and can affect you consciously and subconsciously. Read through the lyrics of the music you are listening to. If the lyrics do not line up with your values, get them out of your life!

Clean house when it comes to the podcasts you listen to. Podcasts can be a very good tool to help you learn while you are driving or exercising. Instead of listening to podcasts for entertainment, try shifting to podcasts that teach you something that will help you get closer to becoming who it is you want to be.

Clean house when it comes to your social media accounts. Social media has become an ego-feeding, spirit-crushing beast for millions of people. If what you consume when you scroll through social media is not feeding your mind or your soul in a positive way, then unfollow, unfriend, block, delete people, delete the entire account—whatever you have to do! Do not be afraid to clean house when it comes to social media. You decide the power you will let it have in your life. Make intentional choices *for* yourself, not against yourself.

> **You are either fueling or depleting your best resources by what you consume.**

Clean out your fridge. I am not kidding. We talked about health back in Chapter 11. What you eat affects your brain, which drives every aspect of how you perform mentally and physically. When you eat bad food, you will get bad results. Most people cannot get their nutrition under control because they are more focused on what they want in the moment versus what they want for their life. Do not risk your meaningful long-term goals for meaningless short-term satisfaction.

You should start cleaning house right away because there is no good reason to put your dreams off any longer. If you want to change your life, you have to intentionally turn your whole environment into a breeding ground for success. It is time to clean house!

#ItFactor

When you start defining your goals, you will discover other people with the same goals as you. You will discover people who have gone before you and who have killed it. Should that stop you from going after it? No! No one will ever be able to fulfill your purpose or live out your passion in the exact way you are meant to. The world needs you to show up and do your thing! No two people are the same, and you have a specific, special gift someone in this world needs to enjoy. Do not rob them of that! Think of it this way: You do not open up the rom-com section of Netflix and see only one movie, right? No way. You see dozens, even hundreds of successful romantic comedies, each with their own spin on it. Do not be afraid of whom your success may be compared to; be afraid of not being true to you.

When it comes to reaching your goals, if you sit idle, it is unforgivable. Regardless of if you have everything or if you came from nothing, only the person willing to take radical action will get to the top. Life will never be effortless. You cannot get what you're not willing to earn. Your work ethic is the "it" factor that will set you apart.

How do you increase your work ethic, your "it" factor?

It boils down to choices. In fact, this whole book boils down to a choice. As you go through your day, ask yourself if what you are doing today, right now, is getting you closer to crushing your goals. If it is not, then stop and change direction. The choices you make will affect you not only today, but the next day and the next day and so on. Work ethic is not something developed in a moment; it is a characteristic that builds over time and absolutely cannot be ignored.

#KeepYourWord

This book captured your attention enough to open it up and start reading. You have made it to this point because something inside you knows that your purpose is deeper and bigger and more meaningful than where you are at right now.

You are worth going all in on this! Do not let go of that hunger deep inside you that was there when you first got this book. Do not let go of the fire ignited in you in this very moment. It is there for a reason! We all have our individual purpose in this life, and until you run as hard as you can toward living that out, you will keep seeking, wishing, wondering, working, searching, and never finding.

Now is your time. It is your turn. Level up and own the full responsibility for making your dreams happen. Put your stake in the ground on this right now. Choose to own it! And I want you to keep your word on this. Make good on this promise to yourself. If you say you are going to do it, do it. Do not change your mind. Do not make excuses. Do not give up. Just do it. Do not live the rest of your life only doing that which you are *able* to do. Instead, choose to do what you were *made* to do! Go out there, level up, and own it!

CONCLUSION

I am a leadership speaker and trainer with Van Hooser Associates, Inc©. I spend my professional life teaching and training leaders at all levels to drive performance and profits through their people. Before writing this book for you, I took time to look at what was already out there to consume for people who want to change their lives.

There are hundreds of thousands of books that will tell you all the things you need to do to change your life. But I did not see the resource that shined a bright light on the part that comes before all the action steps. I did not see the ownership aspect of it all emphasized to the caliber I believe life requires. At the end of the day, most people know what they should do, but they still do not do it. The fact is that it does not matter how much you know—nothing will change for you unless you own the responsibility of leveling up and taking action.

I have poured my heart and soul into this book trying to cut straight through the noise to your heart so that you understand why and how you can own your life. I tried not to put any sugar on it, but if you want the nitty-gritty details of owning it, I am going to sum it up for you plain and simple right here.

Owning it will cost you your comfort zone. It is easy to go with the flow and let other people control your life. There is less thought that goes into life that way. However, do not let your comfort zone rob you of your purpose, passion, and potential.

Owning it creates the power for you to get and become whatever you dream.

Owning it is not a destination; it is a journey. You have the ability to own it, starting right now with every decision you make from this point forward.

Owning it is simple. In every moment, you choose to get closer to your goals rather than farther away.

If you *never* take full ownership of your life, you will end up with unquenchable regret. You will go through the days of your life always starving for something that is missing deep inside. You will throw away your only chance at living out your true calling in this life. You will hand over your story to be written by anyone and anything else that you choose to let be stronger than you.

#YourTurn

If you do not take full responsibility for your life, you likely will never achieve your goals. Instead, when you choose to step up to the plate and make success happen for you—no matter what—you own it. You own your future and you call the shots for what's possible for you. All that's left now is for you to take action.

First step? Close this book and lay down the law (Chapter 2). Dig deep into defining the answers to these questions: Who am I? What do I want? How am I going to get it? *If you text LEVELUP to 66866 I will send you a free worksheet to help.*

Your dreams will be made a reality by how you show up and live your life in every decision, every moment, every day, every week, every month, every year. Choose to *own it*. *Now is your time to level up.*

Acknowledgments

Sometimes words are hard. I know that sounds crazy since I've officially written a book and am a professional speaker, but it feels really true right now as I try to acknowledge all the people who helped make this book a reality.

I have searched for all the right words to say for this first part and maybe I'll come up short, but I'm going to give it my best shot… Writing this book, in many ways, has been like trudging through a huge therapy session for the past several months—really high highs and a couple of pretty low lows. The "therapy" usually went down late at night, as everyone was settling in for bedtime or had already knocked out for the night. Through those late hours, I dug up my past and peeled back the layers of experiences I'd either buried on purpose or simply just forgotten after a while. As I was typing, one word might make a long-forgotten story come to my mind—maybe a story I needed to share with everyone or maybe one I didn't even want to remember. With each memory came emotions…some that I could not turn off when I shut my laptop but that I had to work and pray through for a while. In order to help other people, I had to get this message out to the world…so I did the work.

Through this season of uncovering both the trash and treasure of my prior personal and professional experiences, my husband, as always, was the steady to my shaky ground. Never once did he complain when I woke him up to ask him if I should tell a certain story. Never once did he tell me to be quiet when I spent months talking only about what is holding people back and how much better the world would be if people leveled up, as well as working through naming the exact process of how I did—and how you can—actually crush every goal you have. Every time I opened my mouth he listened. Every time he responded with intentional love and grace and insight. Every time I was reminded just why I said "yes" on 12.31.10. Three kids has felt a little easier than writing this book, honestly. The fact that we made it through this process and when I look in his eyes, I can see he has not been burdened by carrying an extra load while I wrote—he was supportive, he is proud—all of that is just proof that he is without a doubt the single best human being I know. I am so grateful to have him by my side as we elevate our game and crush our goals together. If I had to do this life over again, I'd pick you—15 years sooner—every time. You are the other half of me. I love you, Joe.

Then, my babies. As a working mom, it's really easy to get priorities out of whack without hardly realizing it's happened. For me, family comes first, always. Willow, Lincoln, and Duke…I've purposefully given you a front-row seat to what real work looks like. You lived through the time and effort it takes to reach a goal. You saw sacrifice. And now you see reward. For the rest of your life, this book can be a road map, a tool to show you it can be done, a resource of examples on exactly how to navigate life and crush your dreams. This book may even be what you reach for when you become teenagers and won't ask me directly for my advice anymore. (That's not really going to happen, right? Pinky promise?) To my forever babies, I love you to the moon and back to my heart.

Phil and Susan. I was a teenager when you first said to me that I should write a book. It only took me about 12 years to make it happen…how's that for slowing down for once?! You've both shown me love through encouragement, support, and even tough talks. Fifteen years later, we're in business together, learning and growing from one another. Thank you for the opportunity you've given me with a front-row seat into the speaker/author industry. Your patience, persistence, and encouragement to *just be Alyson* has pushed me to reach even higher. Neither of you has ever treated me as an in-law; you've always treated me as your own. I have no doubt that the Lord goes before us and puts people in our path…we just have to be open enough to see it. I'm so glad that as a sophomore in a high school PE class, I lost my mind over Joe and have been hanging around the Van Hoosers ever since. You all are the best. I'm thankful for incredible ~~in-laws~~ in-loves…Matt & Sarah Wade and Ethan & Sophie Apple, thank you for believing in me and encouraging me. I love you all.

To my parents, without a doubt the biggest driving force in shaping who I am was how I was brought up. I am thankful for what you could give me. It is my hope that this book is an encouragement and even a help to you in your own journey.

Hands down this book would not have happened exactly at this moment in time without Sam Silverstein. Thank you so much for introducing me to Dave. He is as great as you said! And as much as I love and appreciate Sam, I feel the same about his wife, Renee. Thank you both for believing in me right out of the gate. Thank you for sharing encouragement, insight, wisdom, and straight talk. I am blessed by your friendship, personally and professionally.

Dave Wildasin with Sound Wisdom. I wish you could have seen me on the other side of the phone, standing up, sweating bullets, swaying back and forth, as I mustered up every ounce of courage in myself while spewing my vision for this book to you in our first conversation. Whew! You listened. You gave me a chance. Thank you. I don't know how other publishers are, but I'm fortunate enough to find one who is kind, considerate, caring, and incredibly smart. From what I hear, that's rare. I am looking forward to working many more decades and enjoying even bigger successes with you and the Sound Wisdom team.

Nichelle Dunbar. Girl! You saw the earliest draft of this book before anyone else. That was a trip, I'm sure. You're amazing. Thank you for all your help in getting the book to a place I felt I could send to the publisher!

Jen Janechek with Sound Wisdom. One of the first things Dave told me about you was how smart you are. Man, did he hit the nail on the head! I don't know how you do it, but as the editor, you've been able to help capture my voice and make it all grammatically correct—fast! You get me. I've gained a friend throughout this process. Thank you for your tireless work throughout the editing of this manuscript. You encouraged me. You challenged me. You made me better. I am incredibly grateful.

Eileen Rockwell with Sound Wisdom. After one conversation with me about the book you sent back a cover design that I would never have come up with—but that I LOVE! It's modern, sleek, professional, neither masculine nor feminine…I love every aspect of it. Thank you, sincerely. My hope is that your design will be proudly displayed in the hands of professionals around the world for decades to come.

Brian and Karen Walter, Ron and Wendy Culberson, Laurie Guest, Paul ter Wal, Lindsey Adams—this is a group unmatched by most. This past year has been a whole new season of life for me and each of you has welcomed me with open arms. You've offered invaluable guidance. I admire each of you individually as an incredible professional.

You will be special to me forever because of your huge hearts. Thank you for kindness.

Friends and families. The more I thought about it all, the longer the list got…I'm talking 25+ families in western Kentucky alone. I don't want to leave anyone out. If you clothed me, fed me, gave me a ride, provided a roof over my head, loved on me, stuck with me through dark seasons and into brighter ones, considered me "one of yours," cheered me on as I achieved my goals, supported me as I stepped out courageously, and gave me opportunities…thank you. Thank you for walking through this life with me and giving when you had no obligation to. If you're reading this, you know who you are. I love you deeply.

Former bosses, co-workers, employees, and mentors. It's because of working with you that I've learned so much in such a small amount of time. Thank you for teaching, tolerating, and taming a wild 20-something-year-old with a big mouth and even bigger goals. I have a lot more self-control and smarts about myself now at 30 years old. Thank you for the role you played in shaping me into a better person.

I wrote this book to help people. Each of you has played a part in making this a reality. If this book helps one person, you've helped that person. This world can be tough, but life is made better when you find good people—like you—to walk through it with. From the bottom of my heart, thank you.

Love,

Alyson

Meet
Alyson Van Hooser

Alyson Van Hooser has learned a thing or two about the price of admission to success. Tough beginnings unlocked the ownership mindset that she teaches audiences and readers. Alyson passionately believes that with this approach to life and work, you can earn everything you dream of. She has leveled up her personal and professional life through a career in retail, banking, and insurance; as a city councilwoman; young professional of the year; wife and mother of three; and *now* author—all by the age of 30. Now she works with leaders to help them level up in their own personal and professional lives.

Through her work with companies and associations, Alyson speaks and trains leaders at all organizational levels on how to elevate results within themselves and their teams in the 21st-century workforce. Alyson loves inspiring and equipping leaders with practical, tactical approaches to ignite never-before-experienced results. You can learn more about Alyson at vhleadership.com.

Bring Alyson Van Hooser to Your Organization through
Books, Keynotes, & Leadership Development Training

Contact Alyson

hello@vhleadership.com

To order more copies of **Level Up**

or

To get more information on Alyson's latest keynotes or
corporate leadership development training, visit:

alysonvanhooser.com

For more on **Level Up**, check out
www.levelup-thebook.com

Connect with Alyson on Social:

https://www.facebook.com/AlysonVanHooser

https://www.linkedin.com/in/alysonvanhooser/

https://www.instagram.com/alysonvanhooser/